# Data Lakes & Pipelines: A Modern Azure Guide

Kameron Hussain and Frahaan Hussain

Published by Kameron Hussain, 2025.

DATA LAKES & PIPELINES: A MODERN AZURE GUIDE

**First edition. May 21, 2025.**



ISBN: 979-8231336289

Written by Kameron Hussain and Frahaan Hussain.

# Data Lakes & Pipelines: A Modern Azure Guide

**First Edition**

# Preface

The rapid evolution of cloud technologies has fundamentally reshaped the landscape of data architecture. With the explosion of data volume, velocity, and variety, traditional data warehouses have struggled to keep pace. In response, the rise of data lakes and cloud-native analytics platforms has opened up new opportunities for organizations to store, process, govern, and derive value from their data at scale. This book, *Data Lakes & Pipelines: A Modern Azure Guide*, was written to serve as a comprehensive, practical guide to navigating this transformation within the Microsoft Azure ecosystem.

This is the **1st Edition** of the book, and it has been carefully structured to help both novice and experienced data professionals develop a strong understanding of Azure-based data lake architectures, end-to-end pipeline development, security and governance best practices, and integration with machine learning and analytics services.

We begin with foundational topics such as the evolution from traditional warehousing to data lakes and the conceptual model behind Azure Data Lake Storage (ADLS). We explore core components, data classifications, and the architectural principles that guide effective implementation.

From there, we delve into **pipeline design**, covering **ETL**, **ELT**, and **streaming patterns**, while providing hands-on insights into **Azure Data Factory (ADF)** and **Azure Synapse**. We emphasize **performance**, **partitioning strategies**, and the role of **metadata management** using tools like **Azure Purview**. In the realm of

**security**, readers will find in-depth content on **RBAC**, **encryption**, **compliance**, and **lineage** — critical for operating within regulated industries.

Subsequent chapters focus on **workflow orchestration**, **CI/CD practices**, **alerting**, and **error handling** strategies. For those working in **data science and analytics**, we explore the use of **Azure ML**, **Databricks**, and **predictive modeling** within production data pipelines.

The final chapters showcase **real-world architectures**, **IoT scenarios**, **multi-cloud challenges**, and a glimpse into the **future of Azure data engineering**, including **Data Mesh**, **Fabric**, **serverless computing**, and **AI-augmented data workflows**.

This book also includes comprehensive appendices, glossaries, and hands-on projects to help readers apply concepts in practical settings.

Whether you're a data engineer, architect, analyst, or IT leader, this guide will help you build resilient, scalable, and intelligent data platforms using the best of what Azure has to offer. The knowledge in these pages reflects current best practices and anticipates tomorrow's challenges, giving you the tools to innovate confidently in a data-driven world.

# Table of Contents

## Summary

# Chapter 1: Introduction to Data Architecture in the Cloud

## Evolution from Traditional Warehousing to Data Lakes

THE TRADITIONAL DATA warehouse has long been the cornerstone of enterprise analytics. Its structured schema, rigid governance, and performance-optimized architecture made it ideal for business intelligence (BI) use cases. Organizations would extract data from operational systems, transform it to fit a predefined schema, and load it into the warehouse — a model commonly known as ETL (Extract, Transform, Load).

However, over time, the exponential growth in data volume and diversity revealed fundamental limitations in this approach:

- **Rigid schemas** made it difficult to onboard new data sources quickly.
- **Data silos** formed as different departments built their own BI stacks.
- **Limited scalability** created cost and performance bottlenecks.
- **Batch processing delays** meant that insights were always slightly outdated.
- **Inflexibility in handling unstructured data** such as logs, images, and video.

These limitations set the stage for a more flexible, scalable, and cost-effective solution: the **data lake**.

## The Rise of the Data Lake

A DATA LAKE IS A CENTRALIZED repository that allows you to store all your structured and unstructured data at any scale. You can ingest data as-is, without having to first structure it, and run different types of analytics — from dashboards and visualizations to big data processing, real-time analytics, and machine learning — to guide better decisions.

Data lakes are characterized by:

- **Schema-on-read**, rather than schema-on-write.
- **Separation of storage and compute**, enabling scalability.
- **Support for diverse data formats** (CSV, JSON, Parquet, Avro, images, video).
- **Cost-efficient storage**, often in object stores like Azure Blob Storage.
- **High agility**, as new data sources can be added without redesign.

Azure's answer to the data lake challenge is **Azure Data Lake Storage (ADLS)**, a hyperscale storage system built on Azure Blob Storage and enhanced for analytics workloads.

## Data Lakes vs. Traditional Warehouses: A Comparison

| Feature | Traditional Warehouse | Data Lake |
|---|---|---|
| Schema Enforcement | Schema-on-write | Schema-on-read |
| Data Types | Structured only | Structured, semi-structured, unstructured |
| Cost | High (compute-intensive) | Low (object storage) |
| Scalability | Limited | Virtually unlimited |
| Performance | High for structured queries | Optimized via parallel processing |
| Data Governance | Mature tools | Improving rapidly (Purview, RBAC) |
| Use Cases | BI, reporting | ML, big data, real-time, BI |

## The Shift to ELT and Streaming

WITH THE DECOUPLING of storage and compute, cloud-native platforms have enabled new architectural paradigms. The **ELT** (Extract, Load, Transform) pattern emerged as a better fit for scalable data lakes. Raw data is ingested and stored in its native form, and transformations are applied later using scalable compute engines like Azure Synapse or Databricks.

In parallel, **streaming** technologies such as **Azure Event Hubs** and **Stream Analytics** allow for near real-time processing of telemetry, logs, and other time-series data.

This flexibility has enabled businesses to react faster, experiment more freely, and build predictive models using massive volumes of previously untapped data.

## Azure's Data Lake Platform: An Overview

AZURE PROVIDES A COMPREHENSIVE ecosystem for building modern data platforms, including:

- **Azure Data Lake Storage Gen2**: A Hadoop-compatible, scalable object store.
- **Azure Data Factory**: Data integration and orchestration service.
- **Azure Synapse Analytics**: Unified analytics service with data warehousing and big data capabilities.
- **Azure Databricks**: Collaborative Apache Spark-based analytics platform.
- **Azure Stream Analytics**: Real-time data stream processing.
- **Azure Purview**: Data governance and cataloging solution.
- **Azure Machine Learning**: End-to-end MLOps platform.

Each of these services plays a role in the modern data lifecycle — from ingestion and storage to processing, governance, and consumption.

## From Monolith to Modular Data Platforms

THE MOVEMENT FROM CENTRALIZED, monolithic data warehouses to modular, service-based architectures reflects a broader trend in cloud-native engineering:

- **Separation of concerns**: Storage, compute, orchestration, and governance are handled by specialized services.
- **Composable architecture**: Pipelines are assembled from best-of-breed tools.
- **Cloud elasticity**: Scale up or down on demand.
- **Infrastructure as code**: Define and deploy data infrastructure using tools like Terraform or Bicep.
- **Monitoring and observability**: Built-in integration with Azure Monitor and Log Analytics.

Example: Here's a simplified Terraform snippet to provision an Azure Data Lake Storage account:

```
resource "azurerm_storage_account" "datalake" {
name = "mydatalakeacct"
resource_group_name = azurerm_resource_group.main.name
location = azurerm_resource_group.main.location
account_tier = "Standard"
account_replication_type = "LRS"
is_hns_enabled = true # Hierarchical namespace for ADLS Gen2
}
```

This decoupled model allows organizations to evolve their data architecture incrementally, adopt automation and CI/CD pipelines, and align closely with agile delivery models.

## Organizational Impact of Cloud Data Architecture

THE TRANSITION TO DATA lakes and modular cloud platforms is not just technical — it's also cultural and strategic:

- **Data democratization** empowers analysts and data scientists to explore data without waiting for IT to build rigid schemas.
- **Self-service** capabilities reduce operational friction.
- **DevOps and DataOps** cultures enable continuous improvement.
- **Cross-functional collaboration** improves data literacy across departments.

Organizations that embrace these shifts report faster time-to-insight, improved innovation capacity, and better compliance through centralized governance tools.

## Conclusion

THE MOVE FROM TRADITIONAL data warehouses to Azure-based data lakes represents a foundational shift in how organizations store, process, and leverage data. It's not merely a migration — it's a transformation of data strategy, operations, and culture. This section has laid the groundwork for understanding the motivations behind data lake adoption and how Azure supports this paradigm. The chapters that follow will walk through the core components, tools, patterns, and real-world applications to help you build resilient and scalable data platforms using Azure.

# The Role of Azure in Modern Data Infrastructure

THE LANDSCAPE OF DATA infrastructure has undergone a profound transformation driven by the rise of cloud computing, and Microsoft Azure has positioned itself as a central force in this evolution. Azure is not simply a storage platform — it is a full-fledged ecosystem designed to support the entire data lifecycle: from ingestion and storage, to processing, orchestration, governance, analytics, and machine learning. In this section, we explore Azure's capabilities across each of these domains and how they collectively enable the design of robust, scalable, and intelligent data platforms.

## Azure as a Cloud Data Platform

AZURE OFFERS AN EXTENSIVE portfolio of services purpose-built for data workloads, spanning data lakes, warehouses, real-time processing engines, governance frameworks, and AI platforms. Its design principles support the core tenets of modern data infrastructure:

- **Elasticity**: Resources scale automatically to meet demand.
- **Decoupling of Storage and Compute**: Services like Azure Data Lake Storage (ADLS) allow compute resources to operate independently of the storage layer.
- **Pay-as-you-go Pricing**: Optimized for both small teams and large enterprises.
- **Security and Compliance by Design**: Integrated encryption, identity management, and compliance frameworks.
- **Global Availability**: Multi-region deployment with availability zones and geo-redundancy.

## Core Azure Services for Data Infrastructure

THE FOUNDATION OF AZURE'S modern data architecture rests on several core services, each playing a distinct role in the data lifecycle:

### 1. Azure Data Lake Storage (ADLS)

A HYPERSCALE STORAGE service built on Azure Blob Storage, enhanced with hierarchical namespace features for managing directories and files. ADLS Gen2 supports massive volumes of structured and unstructured data, providing the foundation for data lake architectures.

Key features:

- Native HDFS support for compatibility with Hadoop and Spark.
- Fine-grained access control via Azure RBAC and ACLs.
- Integration with analytics tools like Azure Synapse and Databricks.

```
resource "azurerm_storage_data_lake_gen2_filesystem" "example" {

name = "rawdata"

storage_account_id = azurerm_storage_account.example.id

}
```

### 2. Azure Synapse Analytics

A UNIFIED ANALYTICS service that combines data warehousing (SQL-based) with big data analytics (Spark). Synapse allows users to query both relational and non-relational data using T-SQL, Spark, and pipelines in a single workspace.

Use cases:

- Ad hoc analysis and dashboards.
- Large-scale data transformations.
- Data integration from multiple sources.

**3. Azure Data Factory (ADF)**

AZURE'S ETL/ELT ORCHESTRATION tool, ADF is used to build and manage data pipelines that move and transform data between disparate systems. ADF supports over 90 connectors, both on-premises and in the cloud.

Features:

- Code-free visual authoring.
- Integration with Git for version control.
- Data flow transformations using Spark-based runtime.
- Triggers, schedules, and monitoring tools for pipeline orchestration.

**4. Azure Databricks**

A COLLABORATIVE APACHE Spark-based analytics platform optimized for Azure. Databricks simplifies building data lakes and integrating with machine learning workflows. It supports Python, R, Scala, and SQL.

Benefits:

- Auto-scaling clusters.
- MLflow integration for experiment tracking.
- Lakehouse architecture for combining data lakes with ACID transactions (via Delta Lake).

**5. Azure Stream Analytics**

A REAL-TIME ANALYTICS service designed to process large volumes of fast-streaming data. Stream Analytics integrates with Event Hubs, IoT Hub, and Azure Blob Storage, supporting real-time dashboards and anomaly detection scenarios.

Example scenario:

```
SELECT

System.Timestamp AS EventTime,

deviceId,

AVG(temperature) AS AvgTemperature

INTO

outputBlob

FROM

inputStream TIMESTAMP BY eventTime

GROUP BY

TumblingWindow(minute, 5), deviceId
```

### 6. Azure Purview (Now Microsoft Purview)

A UNIFIED DATA GOVERNANCE solution enabling the discovery, cataloging, classification, and lineage tracking of enterprise data. Purview helps organizations comply with regulatory frameworks and improve data literacy across departments.

Key features:

- Automated scanning and classification.
- Custom glossary and metadata management.
- Data lineage visualization.
- Integration with Power BI and ADF.

### 7. Azure Machine Learning

AZURE ML PROVIDES A complete MLOps environment, supporting model training, versioning, deployment, and monitoring. It integrates seamlessly with Azure Data Lake, Synapse, and Databricks, enabling data scientists to operate on live, large-scale datasets.

Capabilities:

- No-code and code-first options.
- AutoML for rapid prototyping.
- Model registry and pipelines.
- Endpoint deployment to Kubernetes or managed inference.

## The Pillars of Azure's Data Architecture

AZURE'S DESIGN IS BASED on architectural principles that align with modern enterprise needs:

### 1. Modularity and Composability

RATHER THAN ENFORCING a monolithic design, Azure allows data teams to compose solutions from individual services. This ensures flexibility and encourages reuse. For instance, a pipeline might ingest data using ADF, store it in ADLS, process it in Databricks, and surface it via Synapse.

### 2. Integration and Interoperability

AZURE'S ECOSYSTEM IS highly integrated. For example:

- ADF pipelines can invoke Databricks notebooks.
- Synapse workspaces can access ADLS directly.
- Azure ML can register features and models to be used in Power BI.

This eliminates the friction between tools and allows for seamless workflows across the data lifecycle.

### 3. Security and Compliance

SECURITY IS FOUNDATIONAL. Azure integrates identity management (Azure Active Directory), fine-grained permissions (RBAC and ACLs), encryption (at rest and in transit), and threat detection (Defender for Cloud). Azure services comply with major frameworks: HIPAA, GDPR, SOC 2, ISO 27001, and more.

For example, encrypting ADLS data with a customer-managed key:

```
resource "azurerm_key_vault_key" "data_lake_key" {
name = "datalake-key"
key_vault_id = azurerm_key_vault.example.id
key_type = "RSA"
key_size = 2048
}
```

**4. Global Reach and Availability**

AZURE OPERATES IN OVER 60 regions worldwide. Services like ADLS and Synapse can be configured for:

- Zone redundancy.
- Geo-redundant storage (GRS).
- Multi-region replication.

This is essential for enterprise-grade availability, data sovereignty, and disaster recovery strategies.

## Common Architectural Patterns Using Azure

MODERN ENTERPRISES commonly adopt the following patterns with Azure services:

**Lakehouse Architecture**

- **Raw data** stored in ADLS.

- **Structured layers** maintained via Delta Lake or Parquet.
- **Databricks** or **Synapse Spark** used for transformation.
- **Power BI** or **Synapse SQL** used for reporting.

**Real-Time Analytics**

- **IoT Hub / Event Hubs** for ingestion.
- **Azure Stream Analytics** or **Databricks Structured Streaming** for processing.
- **Synapse** for aggregations.
- **Dashboarding via Power BI.**

**Machine Learning Workflow**

- DATA IN ADLS.
- Feature engineering in Databricks.
- Model training in Azure ML.
- Deployment to AKS or ACI.
- Monitoring with Application Insights.

## Enterprise Considerations

AZURE ENABLES LARGE-scale implementations with support for:

- **Multi-tenancy** and environment isolation via Resource Groups and Management Groups.

- **Infrastructure-as-Code** via ARM, Bicep, and Terraform.
- **DevOps pipelines** via Azure DevOps or GitHub Actions.
- **Cost management and optimization** with built-in dashboards and budgets.

### Summary

AZURE HAS BECOME ONE of the most comprehensive platforms for building modern data infrastructure. Its services span every stage of the data lifecycle and are designed with scalability, flexibility, security, and integration in mind. The Azure ecosystem empowers data engineers and architects to build intelligent systems that respond in real-time, operate at petabyte scale, and support analytics, AI, and governance from a unified platform.

In the next section, we'll define key terminology and concepts that underpin the Azure data ecosystem, including structured vs. unstructured data, schema-on-read, metadata layers, and the zone-based approach to organizing data lakes. These definitions will provide a shared vocabulary for navigating the rest of the book.

## Key Terminology and Concepts

TO EFFECTIVELY NAVIGATE and implement a modern data infrastructure using Azure, it is crucial to understand the key terminology and conceptual underpinnings that define the architecture, flow, and management of data within the cloud. These concepts are foundational to the practices of data engineering, data architecture, analytics, governance, and security. This section provides a deep dive into the essential terms and principles that will be referenced throughout the rest of the book.

## Data Lake

A **data lake** is a centralized repository that allows you to store all your structured, semi-structured, and unstructured data at any scale. Unlike traditional databases that enforce a strict schema-on-write, data lakes follow a **schema-on-read** approach, meaning data is stored as-is and structured only when it is read or queried.

**Key characteristics:**

- Supports raw, cleansed, and curated data zones.
- Highly scalable and cost-effective.
- Decouples storage and compute.
- Ideal for big data and AI/ML workloads.

## Schema-on-Read vs. Schema-on-Write

- **Schema-on-write**: Data must conform to a predefined schema before it can be stored. Common in traditional RDBMS and data warehouses.
- **Schema-on-read**: Data is stored without a fixed schema and interpreted only when queried or processed. This enables flexibility in handling diverse and evolving data structures.

**Example Scenario:**

- In Azure Data Lake Storage (ADLS), JSON log files from different IoT devices can be stored without needing to define a schema. Later, tools like Synapse or Databricks can apply schema-on-read to process this data.

## Structured, Semi-Structured, and Unstructured Data

UNDERSTANDING THE NATURE of the data being processed is critical when choosing storage, processing engines, and schema management strategies.

- **Structured Data**: Highly organized and easily searchable, typically stored in rows and columns. Example: relational databases (SQL Server, PostgreSQL).

- **Semi-Structured Data**: Contains tags or markers to separate data elements but lacks a rigid schema. Examples include JSON, XML, and Avro.

- **Unstructured Data**: No predefined model. Examples include audio, video, emails, documents, and images.

Azure services like **ADLS**, **Synapse**, and **Databricks** can handle all three types of data efficiently through connectors, parsers, and processing engines.

## Data Ingestion

**DATA INGESTION** refers to the process of collecting and importing data for immediate use or storage in a database, data lake, or warehouse.

**Types of ingestion:**

- **Batch ingestion**: Large volumes of data are ingested at scheduled intervals.

- **Streaming ingestion**: Real-time ingestion of data as it is generated (e.g., IoT sensors, clickstreams).

Azure tools:

- **Batch**: Azure Data Factory (ADF), Synapse Pipelines.
- **Streaming**: Azure Event Hubs, Azure IoT Hub, Azure Stream Analytics.

## ETL vs. ELT

BOTH **ETL (Extract, Transform, Load)** and **ELT (Extract, Load, Transform)** are data integration patterns, but they differ in processing order and compute placement.

- **ETL**:
  - Data is transformed before being loaded into storage.
  - Common in on-premises systems.
  - More processing at the data integration layer.
- **ELT**:
  - Raw data is loaded first, then transformed using the compute capabilities of the target system.
  - Favored in cloud environments due to scalable compute.
  - Supported by Azure Synapse, Databricks, and Snowflake.

**Example ADF ELT Pipeline Structure**:

```
{
"name": "ELT_Pipeline",
"activities": [
```

```
{
"name": "ExtractData",
"type": "Copy",
"inputs": ["SourceDatabase"],
"outputs": ["ADLSRaw"]
},
{
"name": "TransformData",
"type": "DatabricksNotebook",
"notebookPath": "/transformations/cleanse_data"
}
]
}
```

## Data Lake Zones

DATA LAKES ARE TYPICALLY organized into logical zones to enforce processing and governance workflows:

- **Raw Zone**: Stores unprocessed, source-format data.
- **Cleansed Zone**: Data is validated, filtered, and deduplicated.
- **Curated Zone**: Transformed data ready for analytics or ML consumption.

- **Analytics/Consumption Zone** (optional): Optimized for query performance, often stored in columnar formats like Parquet or Delta.

This zoning supports data lineage, traceability, and reprocessing of raw data in case transformation logic changes.

## Data Catalog and Metadata

METADATA IS DATA ABOUT data. In modern data architectures, managing metadata is critical for discovery, governance, and automation.

**Types of metadata:**

- **Technical metadata**: File size, schema, creation timestamp.
- **Business metadata**: Data definitions, glossary terms.
- **Operational metadata**: Data lineage, pipeline performance metrics.

Azure provides **Microsoft Purview** for metadata management, classification, lineage tracking, and cataloging.

**Purview Example**:

- Automatically scans ADLS, Synapse, SQL DB.
- Classifies sensitive data (e.g., PII, PCI).
- Visualizes upstream/downstream lineage for traceability.

## Data Governance

**DATA GOVERNANCE** encompasses the policies, processes, and tools to ensure data is accurate, secure, and used responsibly.

**Key areas:**

- **Access control**: Role-Based Access Control (RBAC), ACLs.
- **Data classification**: Identifying sensitive data.
- **Compliance management**: GDPR, HIPAA, SOC 2.

Azure provides governance features such as:

- **Azure Policy**: Enforce organizational standards.
- **Azure Blueprints**: Define and deploy governance templates.
- **Microsoft Purview**: Centralized governance and cataloging.

## Lineage and Auditing

**DATA LINEAGE** helps track the flow of data from source to destination — essential for troubleshooting, compliance, and reproducibility.

**Auditing** involves logging data access, changes, and pipeline operations to support monitoring and forensic analysis.

Azure tools:

- **Azure Monitor**: Logs and metrics for observability.
- **Log Analytics**: Query platform for diagnostic data.
- **Purview Lineage View**: Visual map of data movement.

## Identity and Access Management (IAM)

ACCESS TO AZURE RESOURCES is controlled using **Azure Active Directory** (**AAD**) and **RBAC**.

- **RBAC (Role-Based Access Control)**: Assigns roles (e.g., Reader, Contributor, Owner) to users/groups at the resource, resource group, or subscription level.

- **Access Control Lists (ACLs)**: File-level permissions in ADLS Gen2 for fine-grained control.

**Example: Assigning Reader Role via Terraform**:

```
resource "azurerm_role_assignment" "data_reader" {

scope = azurerm_storage_account.datalake.id

role_definition_name = "Reader"

principal_id = azuread_user.jane.id

}
```

## Data Processing Engines

AZURE SUPPORTS VARIOUS engines for batch, interactive, and streaming processing:

- **Apache Spark** (Databricks, Synapse): Distributed big data processing.

- **T-SQL** (Synapse SQL Pools): SQL-based data warehousing.

- **U-SQL** (ADLA, legacy): Blend of SQL and C# for big data (now largely deprecated).

- **Kusto Query Language (KQL)**: Used in Azure Data Explorer and Log Analytics.

- **Stream Analytics Query Language**: SQL-like syntax for streaming transformations.

## Data Formats

CHOOSING THE RIGHT data format impacts performance, cost, and usability.

**Common formats:**

- **CSV**: Simple but inefficient for large-scale processing.
- **JSON**: Readable, supports nesting, heavier parsing overhead.
- **Parquet**: Columnar format, great for analytics and compression.
- **Avro**: Row-based, good for serialization and schema evolution.
- **Delta Lake**: Built on Parquet with ACID transactions and versioning.

Databricks, Synapse, and ADF support all major formats, with **Delta Lake** gaining traction for implementing **Lakehouse architectures**.

## Data Virtualization

**DATA VIRTUALIZATION** enables querying external data sources without copying or moving the data.

**Azure Synapse** provides **serverless SQL pools** to query:

- Files in ADLS (e.g., CSV, Parquet).
- External databases (via linked services).
- Data in Cosmos DB, Blob Storage, or Dataverse.

**Example**:

```
SELECT *
FROM OPENROWSET(
```

BULK 'https://mystorageaccount.dfs.core.windows.net/raw/salesdata.parquet',

FORMAT='PARQUET'

) AS [sales];

### Conclusion

MASTERING THESE KEY terms and concepts is essential for any data professional working within the Azure ecosystem. From understanding schema-on-read to implementing lineage-aware governance, these foundational ideas will inform every architecture, design, and implementation decision throughout your journey in building scalable data lakes and intelligent pipelines. These concepts also act as anchors across tools and services, helping bridge the gap between theory and implementation as you move deeper into Azure's modern data platform.

## Target Audience and How to Use This Book

THIS BOOK IS DESIGNED to provide an in-depth yet practical guide to building modern data lake architectures and scalable data pipelines using Microsoft Azure. To make the most of its content, it's important to first understand who this book is for, the various roles it serves, and how different readers can navigate its chapters based on their professional focus, current skill level, and organizational context.

### Who Should Read This Book

WHILE THE TOPIC OF cloud-scale data infrastructure can be vast, this book distills the most critical concepts, tools, and techniques relevant to the following primary audiences:

### Data Engineers

DATA ENGINEERS ARE at the forefront of implementing the architectures described in this book. Topics such as ingestion pipelines, transformation processes, partitioning, orchestration, and storage optimization are central to their day-to-day work. This book provides detailed walkthroughs and Terraform examples for deploying infrastructure, building ETL/ELT pipelines in Azure Data Factory, and managing metadata with Azure Purview.

**What to focus on:**

- Chapters 2 through 6 for core data lake and pipeline construction.
- Chapter 7 for machine learning pipeline integration.
- Chapter 8 for real-world deployment patterns and blueprints.

### Data Architects

DATA ARCHITECTS ARE responsible for defining the high-level design, integration strategy, and governance of data platforms. This book provides architectural diagrams, design principles, and modular patterns for composing scalable, maintainable, and cost-effective Azure-based data ecosystems.

**What to focus on:**

- Chapters 1, 4, and 5 for design principles, governance, and security.
- Chapter 9 for forward-looking insights and emerging paradigms such as Data Mesh and serverless designs.

**Cloud Architects and DevOps Engineers**

AZURE INFRASTRUCTURE provisioning, automation, and cost optimization are crucial for the successful implementation of data platforms. This book provides infrastructure-as-code examples using Terraform and discusses DevOps for data workflows.

**What to focus on:**

- Chapters 4.4, 6.2, and 8 for infrastructure automation and CI/CD practices.
- Appendix 10.3 for sample deployment templates and projects.

**Data Scientists and ML Engineers**

WHILE NOT PRIMARILY targeted at modeling and experimentation, this book highlights how to build production-grade data pipelines and integrate them with Azure ML and Databricks for training, inference, and monitoring. The focus is on operationalizing machine learning within the data infrastructure.

**What to focus on:**

- Chapter 7 for ML pipeline orchestration and model deployment.
- Appendix 10.3 for code examples using MLflow and Azure ML SDK.

**Analysts, BI Developers, and Data Stewards**

ALTHOUGH THIS BOOK is technical in nature, business intelligence professionals and data stewards will benefit from the governance, cataloging, and consumption layer discussions.

Understanding the structure and flow of curated data through lake zones can empower analysts to derive insights more effectively.

**What to focus on:**

- Chapters 2.4 and 5.3 for data zones and lineage.
- Chapter 8.4 for business-focused case studies.

## Skill Levels and Prerequisites

THIS BOOK IS DESIGNED to be accessible to a wide range of readers. However, some foundational knowledge is assumed to maximize the value of the hands-on examples and architectural guidance.

### Beginner

IF YOU'RE NEW TO AZURE or cloud data engineering, this book provides a structured learning path. You'll find clear explanations of concepts such as schema-on-read, lake zones, metadata management, and pipeline orchestration. Practical Terraform snippets, step-by-step instructions for setting up Azure services, and basic examples using Azure Data Factory will help you get started quickly.

**Recommendations:**

- Read chapters in sequential order.
- Use Azure's free tier or sandbox to experiment hands-on.
- Focus on foundational concepts in Chapters 1 through 3.

**Intermediate**

ENGINEERS AND ARCHITECTS with some experience in Azure or other cloud platforms will appreciate the deep dives into optimization, performance tuning, and real-world design patterns. Integration with services like Databricks, Azure ML, and Synapse is explained in detail.

**Recommendations:**

- Jump into performance and orchestration sections in Chapters 4 and 6.
- Use the Terraform modules and automation strategies to standardize deployments.

**Advanced**

ADVANCED READERS WHO are designing enterprise-scale platforms will benefit from the strategic discussions around hybrid cloud, data mesh, and advanced governance. The book does not repeat introductory cloud topics but provides practical implementation guides that can be extended to suit specific enterprise needs.

**Recommendations:**

- Use Chapter 9 to evaluate evolving patterns and prepare for future Azure innovations.
- Leverage the full infrastructure automation approach described in the appendices.

## How to Use This Book in Practice

THIS BOOK IS STRUCTURED to be both **sequentially consumable** and **modular**. Depending on your role, you can either follow the chapters in order to build a comprehensive understanding or skip to the chapters most relevant to your immediate work.

### Recommended Reading Paths

**DATA LAKE BUILDER PATH (Beginner to Intermediate)**:

1. Chapter 1 – Concepts and Context
2. Chapter 2 – Data Lake Fundamentals
3. Chapter 3 – Pipeline Construction
4. Chapter 4 – Scale and Optimization

**DevOps & Automation Path**:

1. Chapter 1.4 – Infrastructure as Code
2. Chapter 6.2 – CI/CD with Azure DevOps
3. Appendix 10.3 – Sample Projects with IaC

**ML Integration Path**:

1. Chapter 7 – Enabling ML Workflows
2. Chapter 3.3 – Databricks Integration
3. Chapter 8.4 – Use Cases and Deployment

**Governance & Compliance Path**:

1. Chapter 5 – Governance and Security
2. Chapter 6.4 – Alerting and Auditing
3. Chapter 9 – Trends and Compliance-Driven Architecture

## Real-World Application Strategy

TO MAXIMIZE YOUR LEARNING and application of this book's content, consider following a **build-test-deploy-govern** approach:

1. **Build**: Use Chapters 2–3 to create a working data lake and ingestion pipeline.
2. **Test**: Validate pipeline logic, schema enforcement, and performance tuning using the tools in Chapter 4.
3. **Deploy**: Automate infrastructure and CI/CD from Chapters 6.2 and the appendices.
4. **Govern**: Apply governance policies using Chapter 5 and Purview features.
5. **Extend**: Integrate ML (Chapter 7) and explore advanced architectures (Chapter 9).

## Learning Environment Setup

THIS BOOK ASSUMES ACCESS to an Azure subscription. For hands-on learning:

- Set up an **Azure Resource Group**.
- Create **Azure Storage Accounts** with hierarchical namespaces.
- Use **Azure Data Factory**, **Databricks**, **Synapse**, and **Purview** within the same region.
- Optionally, provision a **Key Vault**, **Event Hub**, and **Azure ML Workspace**.

**Example Terraform Setup Snippet**:

```
resource "azurerm_resource_group" "main" {
```

```
name = "azure-data-lake-rg"

location = "West Europe"

}

resource "azurerm_storage_account" "datalake" {

name = "datalakestorageacct"

resource_group_name = azurerm_resource_group.main.name

location = azurerm_resource_group.main.location

account_tier = "Standard"

account_replication_type = "LRS"

is_hns_enabled = true

}
```

## Supplemental Resources

EACH CHAPTER INCLUDES:

- **Links to official documentation**
- **Hands-on labs** and project suggestions
- **Reference architectures**
- **Best practices checklists**

In addition, the appendices provide a glossary, cheat sheets, API references, and frequently asked questions, making this a living resource you can refer back to throughout your career.

## Summary

THIS BOOK SERVES AS a strategic and tactical guide to implementing data lake solutions and data pipelines using Microsoft Azure. It caters to data engineers, architects, DevOps professionals, data scientists, and business analysts alike. Whether you're building your first data lake or modernizing an enterprise-scale data platform, this book will equip you with the terminology, architectural guidance, tools, and workflows to execute your vision with confidence. As the Azure ecosystem evolves, the core principles laid out in this book will continue to serve as a durable foundation for modern, intelligent, and resilient data infrastructure.

# Chapter 2: Fundamentals of Data Lakes

## What is a Data Lake?

A **data lake** is a centralized repository designed to store, manage, and analyze vast volumes of raw data in its native format until it is needed. Unlike traditional databases and data warehouses that require upfront schema definitions and tightly controlled data formats, data lakes enable flexible, scalable storage and support for structured, semi-structured, and unstructured data.

At its core, a data lake offers the ability to store everything—logs, images, video, text, JSON, Avro, Parquet, and traditional tabular data—in a single place, accessible via a wide range of analytics and processing tools. This makes data lakes especially powerful in modern cloud architectures where data variety and scale continue to grow exponentially.

### Origins and Purpose

THE CONCEPT OF THE data lake emerged in response to the growing limitations of **schema-on-write** approaches in enterprise data warehousing. These systems required data to be transformed and structured before loading, which led to:

- Increased complexity and cost in data integration.
- High barriers for onboarding new data sources.
- Inflexibility when dealing with evolving schema requirements.

With the explosion of big data, IoT, clickstream, and other non-tabular sources, it became clear that a more adaptable storage model was needed—one that supported **schema-on-read**, deferred transformation, and permitted long-term archival of raw data.

Enter the **data lake**, where raw data is ingested and stored immediately, with downstream applications deciding how and when to interpret it.

## Core Characteristics

THE ESSENTIAL TRAITS of a modern data lake include:

- **Scalability**: Ability to store petabytes of data.
- **Durability**: Backed by object storage services like Azure Data Lake Storage Gen2.
- **Decoupled storage and compute**: Compute services can scale independently of the storage layer.
- **Data format flexibility**: Support for CSV, JSON, XML, Parquet, Avro, images, audio, video, and binary data.
- **Multi-protocol access**: REST, WebHDFS, ABFS, and native integration with Spark, Hive, etc.
- **Fine-grained access control**: Integration with identity providers and policy management tools.
- **Low cost**: Especially for infrequently accessed or archival data.

## Azure Data Lake Storage (ADLS)

AZURE'S DATA LAKE IMPLEMENTATION, **Azure Data Lake Storage Gen2**, is built on top of Azure Blob Storage and includes a **hierarchical namespace** to support file and directory semantics similar to Hadoop Distributed File System (HDFS).

ADLS provides:

- Unlimited storage capacity.
- HDFS-compatible APIs.
- Enterprise-grade security and performance.
- Tight integration with Azure Synapse, Azure Data Factory, Databricks, HDInsight, and other services.

**Terraform Example: Provisioning ADLS**

```
resource "azurerm_storage_account" "adls" {

name = "mystorageaccount"

resource_group_name = "my-resource-group"

location = "East US"

account_tier = "Standard"

account_replication_type = "LRS"

is_hns_enabled = true

}
```

## Data Lake vs. Data Warehouse

WHILE BOTH DATA LAKES and data warehouses are used to store data for analytical purposes, their design philosophies and use cases are significantly different.

| Feature | Data Lake | Data Warehouse |
|---|---|---|
| Schema | Schema-on-read | Schema-on-write |
| Data Types | Structured, semi-structured, unstructured | Structured only |
| Storage Cost | Low (object storage) | High (compute-optimized storage) |
| Processing | ELT, ML, real-time | Traditional BI, OLAP |
| Flexibility | High | Low |
| Use Cases | Big data analytics, AI/ML | Reporting, dashboards |
| Compute Integration | Databricks, Spark, Synapse | SQL engines like Synapse Dedicated SQL |

## Key Components of a Data Lake

TO UNDERSTAND WHAT a data lake is, it's also necessary to examine its components:

### 1. Ingestion Layer

HANDLES IMPORTING DATA from various sources:

- Azure Data Factory
- Event Hubs
- IoT Hub
- Logic Apps
- Azure Synapse Pipelines

Supports both batch and streaming data sources.

**2. Storage Layer**

STORES THE INGESTED data in native format. In Azure, this is typically ADLS Gen2. The storage may be:

- Raw zone (untouched data)
- Cleansed zone (validated and filtered)
- Curated zone (transformed for consumption)

**3. Processing Layer**

TRANSFORMS AND ANALYZES the data using:

- Azure Synapse (SQL + Spark)
- Azure Databricks (Apache Spark)
- Azure Stream Analytics (real-time)
- Azure HDInsight (Hadoop/Spark clusters)

**4. Metadata and Governance Layer**

MANAGES DATA CATALOGING, classification, and lineage:

- Azure Purview (now Microsoft Purview)
- Azure Data Catalog (legacy)
- Tags, labels, and glossary terms

**5. Consumption Layer**

DELIVERS THE DATA TO end users and systems:

- Power BI
- Azure Machine Learning
- APIs and dashboards
- SQL endpoints via Synapse or serverless

## Data Lake Zoning

DATA LAKES OFTEN EMPLOY a zoning strategy to logically separate stages of data transformation:

- **Raw Zone**: Unprocessed data as received from the source systems.
- **Cleansed Zone**: Data has been validated, normalized, and deduplicated.
- **Curated Zone**: Business-specific, high-quality datasets ready for analysis.
- **Analytics Zone**: Aggregated or denormalized data, often stored in performance-optimized formats.

This layered approach enables traceability, reproducibility, and rollback options in case of transformation errors.

## Storage Formats in Data Lakes

THE CHOICE OF STORAGE format significantly impacts performance and interoperability:

| Format | Type | Compression | Use Case |
|---|---|---|---|
| CSV | Row-based | No | Simple tabular data |
| JSON | Semi-structured | No | Logs, configs, flexible schema |
| Parquet | Columnar | Yes | Analytical queries, Synapse, Spark |
| Avro | Row-based | Yes | Streaming, schema evolution |
| Delta | Columnar + ACID | Yes | Databricks Lakehouse, time-travel, merge |

Azure supports native reading of Parquet, Avro, and JSON in Synapse, Databricks, and Data Factory.

## Data Lake Advantages

- **Agility**: Quickly onboard new data sources without heavy ETL.
- **Scale**: Store petabytes without major redesign.
- **Cost-efficiency**: Object storage is inexpensive and durable.
- **Support for ML and AI**: Unstructured data can feed directly into AI models.
- **Future-proof**: Store now, analyze later.

## Limitations and Challenges

DESPITE THEIR FLEXIBILITY, data lakes also come with inherent challenges:

- **Data Swamps**: Without proper governance, a data lake can devolve into a chaotic data dump.

- **Security Complexity**: Fine-grained access control must be implemented with care.

- **Performance**: Querying large volumes of data can be inefficient without partitioning, indexing, or optimized formats.

- **Lineage and Quality**: Tracking data provenance and enforcing quality requires additional tooling (e.g., Purview).

## Best Practices for Designing a Data Lake

- **Start with a clear zone strategy** (raw → curated).

- **Use metadata tagging** for discoverability and classification.

- **Adopt standardized naming conventions** for files, directories, and fields.

- **Implement RBAC and ACLs** early for data protection.

- **Partition and format your data** (e.g., use Parquet with date-based folder structures).

- **Automate pipeline orchestration** with tools like Azure Data Factory and Azure DevOps.

- **Monitor usage and optimize cost** using Azure Cost Management and Log Analytics.

## Conclusion

A DATA LAKE IS FAR more than just a storage bucket—it is the backbone of modern, scalable, cloud-native data platforms. Azure Data Lake Storage provides a powerful foundation to implement these platforms, offering flexibility in data formats, integration with analytic engines, and enterprise-grade security and scalability.

As we progress through the rest of this book, each subsequent chapter will build upon the principles introduced here, demonstrating how Azure services work together to build performant, governed, and intelligent data ecosystems. Understanding what a data lake is—and what it isn't—is critical to achieving success in the cloud data journey.

## Structured vs. Semi-Structured vs. Unstructured Data

DATA LAKES ARE DESIGNED to ingest and store all types of data—structured, semi-structured, and unstructured—at scale and in their native formats. Understanding the differences between these data types is essential to building efficient, scalable, and queryable systems. In this section, we will explore these categories in depth, provide examples of each, examine their implications on storage and processing, and offer guidance on how they are handled within Azure's modern data architecture.

### Structured Data

STRUCTURED DATA IS the most traditionally understood form of data. It resides in fixed fields within records or files, typically organized into tables, columns, and rows. Structured data adheres to a predefined schema that dictates the data types, field names, constraints, and relationships between entities.

**Examples:**

- Relational databases (e.g., SQL Server, PostgreSQL, Oracle).
- Flat files like CSVs with consistent delimiters and field types.
- Tabular exports from ERP, CRM, or finance systems.

**Characteristics:**

- Easily searchable and queryable with SQL.
- Schema-on-write: data must conform to the schema before being stored.
- Relationships between entities are explicitly modeled via foreign keys and indexes.
- Well-suited for reporting, dashboards, and OLAP (Online Analytical Processing).

**Azure Services That Handle Structured Data:**

- **Azure SQL Database**
- **Azure Synapse Analytics (Dedicated SQL Pools)**
- **Azure Data Factory** for extraction and loading
- **Power BI** for consumption

**Example Table Schema (T-SQL):**

```
CREATE TABLE SalesOrders (

OrderID INT PRIMARY KEY,

CustomerID INT,

OrderDate DATE,

TotalAmount DECIMAL(10,2)

);
```

**Use Case:**

Structured data is ideal for repeatable queries such as calculating monthly sales, generating inventory reports, or analyzing customer demographics.

## Semi-Structured Data

SEMI-STRUCTURED DATA does not reside in a traditional row-column structure but contains tags or markers to separate data elements. It supports hierarchical or nested structures, and while it is not rigidly defined, it still maintains organizational properties that make it partially queryable and indexable.

**Examples:**

- JSON documents
- XML files
- YAML and Avro
- Parquet (columnar and typed)
- Log files with consistent formats

**Characteristics:**

- Schema-on-read: structure is inferred at query or processing time.
- Supports nesting and arrays.
- Flexible and self-describing (e.g., key-value pairs).
- Great for APIs, logs, telemetry, and hierarchical data models.

**Azure Services That Handle Semi-Structured Data:**

- **Azure Data Lake Storage Gen2** (raw storage)

- **Azure Synapse Analytics (Serverless SQL)** for schema-on-read querying
- **Azure Databricks** (Spark-based transformations)
- **Azure Stream Analytics** (log and event processing)
- **Azure Cosmos DB** (for operational use cases)

**Example JSON Document:**

```
{
"orderId": 12345,
"customer": {
"id": 789,
"name": "Jane Doe"
},
"items": [
{ "productId": 1, "quantity": 2 },
{ "productId": 3, "quantity": 1 }
],
"totalAmount": 99.99
}
```

**Querying JSON in Azure Synapse (Serverless SQL):**

```
SELECT
JSON_VALUE(doc, '$.orderId') AS OrderID,
```

```
JSON_VALUE(doc, '$.customer.name') AS CustomerName

FROM

OPENROWSET(

BULK 'https://mydatalake.dfs.core.windows.net/raw/orders/*.json',

FORMAT='CSV',

FIELDTERMINATOR ='0x0b',

FIELDQUOTE = '0x0b'

) WITH (doc NVARCHAR(MAX)) AS orders;
```

**Use Case:**

Semi-structured data is perfect for flexible, evolving schemas such as API responses, e-commerce event tracking, IoT telemetry, or configuration data.

## Unstructured Data

UNSTRUCTURED DATA REFERS to information that lacks a predefined format or schema. It cannot be stored in traditional row-column databases and often requires specialized processing to derive structure or meaning.

**Examples:**

- Audio files
- Video streams
- Images (JPG, PNG, TIFF)

- PDFs and Office documents
- Scanned forms
- Emails and free-form text
- Social media content

**Characteristics:**

- Cannot be queried directly using SQL without pre-processing.
- Requires metadata extraction, content indexing, or machine learning.
- Stored in binary or blob format.
- Often large in size (megabytes to terabytes).

**Azure Services That Handle Unstructured Data:**

- **Azure Data Lake Storage Gen2** and **Blob Storage**
- **Azure Cognitive Services** (vision, language, speech processing)
- **Azure Search** for indexing and querying document content
- **Azure Media Services** for video encoding and streaming
- **Azure Form Recognizer** and **Computer Vision API**

**Example:**

A folder in ADLS may contain thousands of scanned receipts in PDF format. Azure Form Recognizer can be used to extract fields like invoice number, date, total, and vendor name and output structured JSON.

**Use Case:**

Unstructured data is typically used in analytics for customer behavior, sentiment analysis, OCR from documents, facial recognition, or training AI models.

## Differences in Storage and Processing Strategies

| Feature | Structured | Semi-Structured | Unstructured |
|---|---|---|---|
| Format | Tables, CSV | JSON, XML, Avro, Parquet | PDF, audio, image, video |
| Queryability | High | Medium (via parsing) | Low (needs processing) |
| Storage Type | Databases, Tables | Files with metadata | Binary blobs |
| Schema | Predefined | Flexible | None |
| Storage in ADLS | Parquet, CSV | JSON, Avro, Parquet | Binary files |
| Analytics Readiness | Immediate | Needs parsing | Needs extraction |
| Tools | SQL Server, Synapse | Databricks, Serverless SQL | Cognitive Services, ML |

## Challenges and Solutions

### STRUCTURED DATA CHALLENGES:

- Rigid schema evolution.
- Data model drift over time.
- High up-front data modeling effort.

**Solutions:**

- Data warehouse automation tools.

- Slowly Changing Dimensions (SCD) patterns.
- Use of lakehouse architecture to blend flexibility.

**Semi-Structured Data Challenges:**

- Parsing overhead.
- Inconsistent key presence across records.
- Complex joins and transformations.

**Solutions:**

- Use Parquet or Delta to convert JSON to optimized format.
- Flatten nested structures using Data Flow in ADF or Spark.

**Unstructured Data Challenges:**

- Lack of queryability.
- Large file sizes.
- Need for metadata enrichment and ML processing.

**Solutions:**

- Index content using Azure Search.
- Use Form Recognizer for document intelligence.
- Extract tags with Azure Cognitive Services.

## Schema Management Approaches

- **Schema Evolution**: Delta Lake and Avro support schema evolution during writes.

- **Schema Inference**: Tools like Spark and Serverless SQL Pools can auto-infer structure.

- **Schema Enforcement**: Structured data requires consistent typing; semi-structured can enforce optional contracts via tools like Azure Data Schema Registry.

## Best Practices

- CHOOSE FILE FORMATS based on usage: **Parquet** for analytics, **JSON** for flexibility, **CSV** for compatibility.

- Partition semi-structured data based on timestamps or categories.

- Always store unstructured data in **append-only** or **immutable** buckets to simplify lineage and recovery.

- Apply **metadata tagging** consistently for all three data types.

- Convert frequently accessed semi-structured data to **Delta format** for performance.

## Conclusion

UNDERSTANDING STRUCTURED, semi-structured, and unstructured data types is fundamental when designing data lakes on Azure. Each type demands different storage strategies, processing tools, and governance approaches. Azure's ecosystem is uniquely capable of handling this diversity through services like ADLS Gen2, Databricks, Synapse, and Cognitive Services. By strategically aligning tools with data types, architects and engineers can create unified platforms that ingest, store, govern, and analyze any form of data with confidence and agility. The next section explores how Azure Data Lake Storage (ADLS) provides the technical foundation for achieving this vision.

# Core Components of Azure Data Lake Storage (ADLS)

AZURE DATA LAKE STORAGE (ADLS) is a foundational service for building modern, scalable data lake architectures in the cloud. It is a highly scalable and secure data lake service built on top of Azure Blob Storage that combines the best of both data lakes and cloud object stores. ADLS enables organizations to store all types of data—structured, semi-structured, and unstructured—at virtually unlimited scale and at low cost, with strong integration to the rest of the Azure data and analytics ecosystem.

This section explores the architecture, capabilities, and core components of ADLS, providing a comprehensive understanding of how it fits into enterprise data platforms and how to effectively configure and use it.

## Overview of ADLS Architecture

AZURE DATA LAKE STORAGE Gen2 is built on Azure Blob Storage and extends its capabilities by adding:

- A **hierarchical namespace** (HNS) for organizing files and directories.
- Fine-grained **access control** using POSIX-like ACLs.
- Native **HDFS compatibility**, enabling big data processing engines to work with ADLS as if it were a local file system.
- Optimized performance for analytics workloads with high-throughput data access patterns.

By combining these features, ADLS becomes a powerful and flexible foundation for modern data lakes and big data platforms.

## Key Components

THE FOLLOWING ARE THE core architectural components and configuration options of ADLS that support its power and versatility:

### 1. Storage Account

ALL DATA STORED IN ADLS resides in an **Azure Storage Account**. To enable data lake features, the storage account must be created with the **Hierarchical Namespace** property enabled.

**Properties:**

- Unique name within Azure.
- Location/region.
- Performance tier (Standard or Premium).
- Redundancy options (LRS, ZRS, GRS, RA-GRS).

**Terraform Example:**

```
resource "azurerm_storage_account" "adls" {

name = "mydatalakestorage"

resource_group_name = azurerm_resource_group.main.name

location = azurerm_resource_group.main.location

account_tier = "Standard"

account_replication_type = "LRS"

is_hns_enabled = true
```

}

## 2. Hierarchical Namespace (HNS)

A HIERARCHICAL NAMESPACE allows files and directories to be organized into a structured tree, similar to traditional file systems. This brings several benefits over a flat namespace:

- Faster renaming and deletion of folders.
- Better support for fine-grained security (file- and folder-level ACLs).
- Enhanced metadata tracking and performance for big data operations.

**Example Structure:**

/raw/2024/01/events.json

/curated/sales/2024/q1/report.parquet

/logs/app/webserver/2024-01-01.log

This file/folder approach aligns well with data lake zoning strategies (raw → cleansed → curated).

## 3. Containers (File Systems)

IN ADLS GEN2, CONTAINERS act like root directories (file systems) within the storage account. Each container can hold a hierarchy of directories and files.

**Purpose:**

- Logical separation of data domains.

- Granular access control boundaries.
- Multi-tenant isolation within the same account.

**Example Terraform Resource:**

```
resource "azurerm_storage_data_lake_gen2_filesystem" "raw_zone" {

name = "raw"

storage_account_id = azurerm_storage_account.adls.id

}
```

Common containers:

- raw
- cleansed
- curated
- sandbox
- logs

### 4. Directories and Files

INSIDE CONTAINERS, data is organized into **directories** and **files**. These can be programmatically created, accessed, and managed via REST APIs, SDKs, or tools like Azure CLI, PowerShell, or Python.

**Use cases:**

- Organizing files by ingestion date, data source, or department.
- Partitioning data by year/month/day for efficient processing.

- Storing schema files, metadata, and documentation.

**Example CLI:**

az storage fs directory create—account-name mydatalakestorage—name "curated/sales/2024"—file-system curated

**5. Access Control Mechanisms**

ADLS SUPPORTS **RBAC** (Role-Based Access Control) and **POSIX-compliant ACLs** (Access Control Lists). These security layers ensure both administrative and granular file access permissions.

**RBAC Roles:**

- Storage Blob Data Reader
- Storage Blob Data Contributor
- Storage Blob Data Owner

**POSIX ACLs:**

Set at the file or directory level using Azure CLI or SDK.

**Example:**

az storage fs access set—acl "user::rwx,group::r—,other::—-" \

—path "curated/sales/2024" \

—account-name mydatalakestorage \

—file-system curated

Benefits:

- Combine RBAC and ACLs for layered security.
- Enforce principle of least privilege.
- Define inheritance for directories to auto-apply permissions.

### 6. Data Redundancy and Availability

AZURE PROVIDES MULTIPLE options for redundancy to meet durability and disaster recovery needs:

- **LRS (Locally Redundant Storage)**: Replicates data within a single data center.
- **ZRS (Zone-Redundant Storage)**: Replicates data across multiple availability zones.
- **GRS (Geo-Redundant Storage)**: Replicates data to a secondary region.
- **RA-GRS**: GRS with read access to the secondary region.

Choose based on business continuity, compliance, and RTO/RPO requirements.

### 7. Integration with Azure Ecosystem

ADLS IS TIGHTLY INTEGRATED with virtually every Azure data and AI service:

- **Azure Synapse**: Query files directly using T-SQL or Spark.
- **Azure Databricks**: Mount ADLS containers using ABFS.
- **Azure Data Factory**: Use as both source and sink in data pipelines.

- **Azure Machine Learning**: Train models on data stored in ADLS.
- **Azure Purview**: Automatically scan and catalog ADLS contents.

**Synapse Example:**

```
SELECT *

FROM OPENROWSET(

BULK 'https://mydatalakestorage.dfs.core.windows.net/curated/sales/2024/report.parquet',

FORMAT = 'PARQUET'

) AS sales_data;
```

**8. Monitoring and Diagnostics**

MONITORING TOOLS INCLUDE:

- **Azure Monitor**: Alerts, metrics, logs.
- **Log Analytics**: Custom queries on operations and access.
- **Storage Metrics**: Transaction count, ingress/egress, latency.
- **Azure Advisor**: Cost optimization and performance insights.

Example metrics to track:

- Blob read/write operations.
- API latency.
- Data egress volumes.
- Access failure rates (403/404).

**Example Query in Log Analytics:**

```
StorageBlobLogs

| where AccountName == "mydatalakestorage"

| summarize Count = count() by HttpStatusCode
```

**9. Performance Optimization Features**

- **Partitioning**: Store files in folders named by time or business dimension (/year=2024/month=01/).
- **Format Selection**: Use columnar formats like Parquet for analytical queries.
- **Parallelism**: ADLS supports concurrent access and batch operations.
- **Caching**: Azure Synapse and Databricks support caching of frequently accessed data.

Best practices:

- Avoid too many small files (metadata overhead).
- Compress large files.
- Use folder structures that align with query patterns.

**10. Data Lifecycle Management**

ADLS SUPPORTS **lifecycle policies** to automatically transition or delete data based on age or access pattern.

**Example Policy:**

- Move blobs to cool tier after 30 days.
- Delete blobs after 180 days.

**Configuration via Azure Portal or ARM Template.**

Benefits:

- Optimize cost by tiering infrequently used data.
- Automate archival and deletion policies.
- Ensure compliance with retention policies.

## Security and Compliance Features

- **Encryption at Rest**: Enabled by default using Microsoft-managed or customer-managed keys (CMK via Key Vault).
- **Private Endpoints**: Restrict access to resources within a virtual network.
- **Firewall Rules**: Limit access by IP ranges.
- **TLS Enforcement**: Encrypted data transmission by default.
- **Compliance**: ADLS meets standards including HIPAA, GDPR, ISO 27001, FedRAMP.

**Key Vault Integration Example (Terraform):**

```
resource "azurerm_key_vault_key" "cmk" {

name = "adls-key"

key_vault_id = azurerm_key_vault.main.id

key_type = "RSA"
```

```
key_size = 2048

}
```

## Summary

AZURE DATA LAKE STORAGE (ADLS) is the core engine behind Azure's data lake strategy. Its scalable architecture, native HDFS support, hierarchical namespace, security model, and deep integration with Azure services make it the ideal backbone for storing and processing massive volumes of diverse data. Whether you're implementing real-time analytics, machine learning workflows, or complex ETL pipelines, understanding the components of ADLS—and how to configure them—will be instrumental in building performant, secure, and cost-efficient data platforms.

The next section will cover how data lakes are logically organized using zoning principles—raw, cleansed, and curated layers—and how these zones support governance, reusability, and pipeline architecture.

# Data Lake Zones: Raw, Cleansed, Curated

THE IMPLEMENTATION of a successful data lake architecture on Azure relies heavily on the logical organization of data into distinct **zones**. These zones define the lifecycle stages of data as it moves from raw ingestion to being ready for analytics or machine learning. Organizing data into zones improves manageability, traceability, security, and operational efficiency. In Azure Data Lake Storage (ADLS), this is typically achieved using well-defined directory structures, naming conventions, access control policies, and lifecycle management rules.

This section explores the purpose, structure, best practices, and practical application of the most common data lake zones: **Raw**, **Cleansed**, and **Curated**. We will also touch on extended zones such as **Sandbox**, **Analytics**, and **Quarantine** used in more advanced implementations.

## The Importance of Zoning in a Data Lake

BEFORE DIVING INTO the specific zones, it's important to understand why zoning is used:

- **Governance**: Different zones have different access, retention, and security rules.
- **Modularity**: Enables independent teams to work on ingestion, transformation, and analytics.
- **Reproducibility**: Retaining raw data allows reprocessing with improved logic over time.
- **Auditing and Lineage**: Changes are tracked from source to consumption.
- **Cost Management**: Lifecycle policies can manage cold storage or deletion.
- **Pipeline Design**: Logical separation supports modular, orchestrated data pipelines.

Zones are implemented as **directories or containers** within ADLS Gen2, and each zone has its own sub-structure based on time, data source, or business function.

## Raw Zone

**PURPOSE**: Store data in its original, unprocessed format exactly as received from the source system.

This zone is a **write-only area** used for:

- Compliance and auditability.
- Reprocessing and rollback.
- Lineage validation.
- Debugging data ingestion issues.

**Data Characteristics**:

- No schema enforcement.
- Possible duplicates or incomplete records.
- Often includes multiple file formats.

**Typical Structure**:

/raw/source_system_name/year=2025/month=01/day=12/

**Best Practices**:

- Automate folder partitioning using ingestion timestamp.
- Store files in original format (e.g., CSV, JSON, XML).
- Restrict access to ingestion pipelines only.
- Avoid modifying or deleting files post-ingestion.

**Terraform Snippet**:

```
resource "azurerm_storage_data_lake_gen2_path" "raw_iot" {
```

```
path = "raw/iot_sensors/year=2025/month=01"

filesystem_name                                                =
azurerm_storage_data_lake_gen2_filesystem.raw.name

storage_account_id = azurerm_storage_account.adls.id

resource = "directory"

}
```

## Cleansed Zone

**PURPOSE**: Hold validated, deduplicated, and transformed data. This is the first zone where data quality rules, schema normalization, and lightweight transformations are applied.

**Data Characteristics**:

- Consistent schema (normalized).
- Clean field names, correct data types.
- Removal of PII or sensitive values (if required).
- Enriched with technical metadata (e.g., ingestion timestamp, source system ID).

**Use Cases**:

- Intermediate state for transformation.
- Input for curated data models.
- Staging area for Data Quality checks.

**Typical Structure**:

/cleansed/domain/entity/year=2025/month=01/day=12/

**Transformation Examples**:

- Remove duplicate records based on business key.
- Standardize date formats.
- Convert string-based numbers to numeric types.
- Normalize field names: OrderDate → order_date.

**Recommended Format**:

Use **Parquet** or **Avro** for optimized performance and compression.

**Security Practices**:

- Broader access than raw zone, but still restricted.
- Role separation for data engineers and analysts.

**ADF Mapping Data Flow Example**:

```
{
"source": "raw/orders/*.json",
"sink": "cleansed/orders/2025/01/",
"transformations": [
"remove_duplicates(order_id)",
"convert(order_date, 'yyyy-MM-dd')",
"derive(column='load_timestamp', expression='currentUTC()')"
]
```

```
}
```

## Curated Zone

**PURPOSE**: Store business-ready data that is trusted, structured, and optimized for analytics or data science.

This is the **gold layer**—the final state of data for most consumers.

**Data Characteristics**:

- Clean, modeled, and enriched.
- Includes derived columns (e.g., customer segment).
- High-quality, ready for dashboards or ML models.
- Used for KPIs and operational reporting.

**Use Cases**:

- Power BI dashboards.
- Azure Machine Learning training pipelines.
- External API outputs.
- Ad hoc SQL querying in Synapse.

**Typical Structure**:

/curated/domain/table_name/version=1/

**Modeling Examples**:

- Fact and dimension tables for star/snowflake schemas.
- SCD Type 2 implementations (historical tracking).

- Aggregates and materialized views.

**Data Format**:

Use **Delta Lake**, **Parquet**, or **Synapse-dedicated tables** for optimal performance and transactional support.

**Access Control**:

- Read access granted to analysts, scientists, and application developers.
- Write access restricted to transformation processes.

**Versioning and Auditability**:

- Maintain dataset versions for reproducibility.
- Log transformation logic in metadata catalog (e.g., Azure Purview).

**Databricks Notebook Snippet**:

```
df = spark.read.parquet("/cleansed/sales/2025/01/")

df_clean = df.withColumn("revenue", df["quantity"] * df["unit_price"])

df_clean.write.format("delta").mode("overwrite").save("/curated/sales/monthly")
```

## Optional Zones

ADVANCED DATA LAKES may include additional zones for operational or exploratory needs.

**Sandbox Zone**

USED BY DATA SCIENTISTS or analysts for prototyping:

- Unrestricted read/write access (with governance).
- Allows exploration and hypothesis testing.
- Periodically cleaned or reset.

Structure:

/sandbox/user/jane.doe/experiment_01/

**Analytics Zone**

SERVES BI TOOLS AND semantic models:

- Aggregated, denormalized datasets.
- Optimized for visualizations and fast filtering.

Structure:

/analytics/domain/dashboard_name/

**Quarantine Zone**

ISOLATES CORRUPTED, malformed, or non-compliant files:

- Ingestion failures, schema mismatches.
- Manual or automated review.
- Retained for a limited time.

Structure:

/quarantine/source=finance/batch_id=20250101/

---

## Governance Across Zones

| Zone | Access Level | Retention Policy | Purpose |
|---|---|---|---|
| Raw | Restricted (write) | Long-term archive | Original data for lineage & reprocessing |
| Cleansed | Data Engineers | Medium-term | Clean data, intermediate format |
| Curated | Analysts, Apps | Short/long-term | Trusted, query-ready datasets |
| Sandbox | Individual Users | Ephemeral | Experimentation and prototyping |
| Quarantine | Data Engineers | Short-term | Isolated data issues |

GOVERNANCE MECHANISMS:

- **Azure Purview** for lineage and classification.
- **Azure Policies** for zone-level data retention.
- **RBAC and ACLs** for access control per zone.
- **Tagging and metadata standards** to label datasets with zone classification.

---

## Lifecycle Automation

AZURE SUPPORTS AUTOMATION of lifecycle transitions using rules and pipelines:

- Move data from raw → cleansed via Azure Data Factory.

- Trigger Spark jobs to convert cleansed → curated.
- Archive or delete based on age in raw/cleansed.

**ADF Pipeline Outline**:

- **Trigger**: New file in raw zone.
- **Stage 1**: Validate schema and deduplicate.
- **Stage 2**: Standardize and transform.
- **Stage 3**: Write to curated zone in Parquet format.

**Example Azure CLI Lifecycle Rule**:

az storage account management-policy create \

—account-name mystorageacct \

—policy @policy.json

**policy.json** could define rules such as:

- Move to Cool tier after 30 days.
- Delete after 180 days in raw zone.

---

## Summary

DATA LAKE ZONING PROVIDES a systematic framework to manage the flow, quality, and usability of data in Azure Data Lake Storage. The raw, cleansed, and curated zones each serve a specific purpose in the data lifecycle, from initial ingestion to final consumption. By adopting zoning strategies, organizations can ensure that their data pipelines are modular, auditable, and governed. This structure also simplifies team responsibilities, data discovery, cost management, and compliance.

In the next chapter, we will explore how to design scalable pipelines that leverage these zones effectively—transforming data as it travels from ingestion through to business insights.

# Chapter 3: Building Scalable Data Pipelines

## Pipeline Concepts: ETL, ELT, and Streaming

DATA PIPELINES ARE the lifeblood of modern data platforms. They ingest, transform, and deliver data from a wide variety of sources to consumers such as data warehouses, analytics tools, machine learning models, and downstream applications. In cloud environments like Microsoft Azure, pipelines must be designed to handle massive volumes of data, support diverse data types, ensure data quality, and scale efficiently as workloads grow.

This section provides a deep dive into three core paradigms of data pipelines—**ETL (Extract, Transform, Load)**, **ELT (Extract, Load, Transform)**, and **Streaming**—with a specific focus on how they are implemented in Azure. We will examine the principles, design considerations, advantages, and limitations of each model, along with best practices for scalability and reliability.

---

### Understanding the Lifecycle of a Data Pipeline

REGARDLESS OF THE PARADIGM used, all pipelines generally follow a three-phase lifecycle:

1. **Extract**: Capture data from source systems—databases, APIs, logs, files, sensors, etc.
2. **Transform**: Clean, enrich, join, and reformat data for analysis or application use.
3. **Load**: Deliver transformed data to the target storage—data lake, data warehouse, operational database, or API.

What differentiates ETL, ELT, and Streaming lies in **when and where transformations happen**, and whether the data is handled in **batch** or **real-time**.

---

## ETL (Extract, Transform, Load)

ETL IS THE TRADITIONAL data integration pattern used in data warehouses and BI systems. The process consists of extracting data from source systems, transforming it in a staging area or transformation engine, and then loading the final dataset into the destination.

**Key Characteristics:**

- Transformations are performed before loading into the destination.
- Transformation logic resides in ETL tools or dedicated compute services.
- Typically used for nightly or hourly batch processes.

**Common Tools in Azure:**

- **Azure Data Factory** (Mapping Data Flows)
- **SQL Server Integration Services (SSIS)**
- **Azure Functions** (for custom transformations)

**Use Cases:**

- Moving ERP and CRM data into Synapse SQL Pools.
- Generating data marts for Power BI.
- Historical trend analysis.

**Advantages:**

- Reduces load on the target system.
- Ensures only clean data is loaded.
- Easier to apply complex transformation logic in a centralized service.

**Challenges:**

- Longer latency.
- Higher operational complexity.
- Transformation logic may be tightly coupled to pipeline infrastructure.

**ADF ETL Pipeline Example (Pseudocode):**

```
{
"name": "ETL_Pipeline",
"activities": [
{
"type": "Copy",
"source": "SQLServerDB",
"sink": "StagingBlob"
},
{
"type": "MappingDataFlow",
```

```
"name": "TransformData"
},
{
"type": "Copy",
"source": "TransformedBlob",
"sink": "SynapseDataWarehouse"
}
]
}
```

## ELT (Extract, Load, Transform)

ELT IS THE DOMINANT pattern in cloud-native data architectures, especially when working with scalable data lakes and powerful compute engines like Azure Synapse or Databricks. Here, raw data is first loaded into a central repository (e.g., ADLS), and transformations are performed afterwards.

**Key Characteristics:**

- Load comes before transformation.
- Compute-intensive tasks are offloaded to scalable engines like Spark or T-SQL.
- Ideal for schema-on-read and flexible analytics.

**Azure Services Used:**

- **Azure Synapse Analytics** (Serverless and Dedicated Pools)

- **Azure Databricks**
- **Delta Lake** (for ACID transaction support)

**Use Cases:**

- Building curated zones from raw data lakes.
- Ad hoc data exploration.
- ML model training pipelines.

**Advantages:**

- Faster ingestion (raw data lands quickly).
- Supports iterative, on-demand transformations.
- Decouples data ingestion from business logic.

**Challenges:**

- Requires robust governance of raw data.
- May increase storage footprint temporarily.
- Risk of "data swamp" if not curated properly.

**Databricks ELT Example (PySpark):**

```
df_raw = spark.read.json("/raw/iot/events/2025/05/12")

df_clean = df_raw.filter("temperature IS NOT NULL")

df_enriched = df_clean.withColumn("event_hour", hour(df_clean["timestamp"]))

df_enriched.write.mode("overwrite").parquet("/curated/iot/hourly/")
```

**Serverless SQL ELT Example:**

```
SELECT *

INTO curated.sales_transformed

FROM OPENROWSET(

BULK 'https://mydatalake.dfs.core.windows.net/raw/sales/2025/*.parquet',

FORMAT = 'PARQUET'

) AS raw_data

WHERE raw_data.sale_amount > 0;
```

## Streaming Pipelines

STREAMING PIPELINES process data **in real time or near-real time** as it arrives. This model is essential for time-sensitive scenarios such as anomaly detection, real-time dashboards, fraud detection, or IoT telemetry.

**Key Characteristics:**

- Data is processed as soon as it arrives.
- Low-latency processing and delivery.
- Event-driven rather than scheduled.

**Azure Tools for Streaming:**

- **Azure Stream Analytics**
- **Azure Event Hubs**

- **Azure Databricks Structured Streaming**
- **Azure Synapse Streaming Pipelines**

**Use Cases:**

- Real-time monitoring of manufacturing sensors.
- Live tracking of logistics and delivery.
- Alerting on fraud patterns in financial transactions.

**Advantages:**

- Instant insights and decisions.
- Handles continuous streams of data.
- Enables reactive, automated systems.

**Challenges:**

- Requires robust failure handling and checkpointing.
- May be harder to debug and backfill.
- Consistency and ordering must be managed.

**Stream Analytics SQL Example:**

```
SELECT

deviceId,

AVG(temperature) AS avg_temp,

System.Timestamp AS window_end

INTO
```

```
curated.iot_temperature
FROM
iot_input TIMESTAMP BY time
GROUP BY
TumblingWindow(minute, 5),
deviceId
```

**Structured Streaming in Databricks:**

```
stream_df = (
spark.readStream
.format("eventhubs")
.options(**eh_config)
.load()
)
parsed_df = stream_df.selectExpr("cast(body as string) as json").select(from_json("json", schema).alias("data"))
parsed_df.writeStream.format("delta").option("checkpointLocation", "/checkpoints/iot/").start("/curated/iot/")
```

## Comparing ETL, ELT, and Streaming

| Feature | ETL | ELT | Streaming |
|---|---|---|---|
| Transformation Location | Before load (middle tier) | After load (in data lake) | Real-time on ingestion |
| Ideal Storage | Data warehouse | Data lake | Event hub / real-time tables |
| Latency | High | Medium | Low |
| Flexibility | Medium | High | Medium |
| Scalability | Low to medium | High | High |
| Tooling (Azure) | ADF, SSIS | Synapse, Databricks | Event Hubs, Stream Analytics |
| Use Case Examples | BI reports, compliance | ML, advanced analytics | IoT monitoring, fraud detection |

## Designing for Scalability and Resilience

TO ENSURE DATA PIPELINES can scale with organizational growth and data volume, consider the following:

1. **Decouple ingestion and transformation** to isolate failures and allow parallelization.
2. **Use partitioning and file formats** like Parquet to minimize scan time and optimize read performance.
3. **Implement idempotent transformations** so that reprocessing the same data does not produce duplicates.
4. **Adopt DataOps practices**, including version control, CI/CD for pipeline deployment, and unit testing for transformations.
5. **Add monitoring and alerting** using Azure Monitor, Log Analytics, and pipeline failure triggers.
6. **Use schema evolution handling** (e.g., Delta Lake) for

pipelines that process semi-structured or changing data.

---

## Infrastructure as Code (IaC) for Pipelines

DEFINING PIPELINES as code enables repeatable deployment and environment consistency.

**Example Terraform Snippet for ADF Pipeline:**

```
resource "azurerm_data_factory_pipeline" "example" {

name = "etl_pipeline"

data_factory_id = azurerm_data_factory.example.id

activities_json = file("pipelines/etl_pipeline.json")

}
```

**Benefits:**

- Enables version control and peer reviews.
- Supports automated testing and deployment.
- Promotes consistency across environments.

---

## Summary

THE ABILITY TO BUILD flexible, scalable, and reliable data pipelines is essential for modern data platforms. ETL, ELT, and Streaming each offer distinct approaches to data movement and transformation, with trade-offs between latency, complexity, and scalability. Azure provides a rich ecosystem to support all three paradigms, allowing teams to choose the best-fit model for their data and business requirements.

As we move forward, the next sections of this chapter will explore the tools Azure provides to implement these pipelines—starting with Azure Data Factory, the backbone of batch-oriented data integration and orchestration on the Azure platform.

## Azure Data Factory (ADF) Essentials

AZURE DATA FACTORY (ADF) is a fully managed, cloud-based data integration service that enables you to orchestrate and automate data movement and transformation at scale. As the centerpiece of Azure's data pipeline ecosystem, ADF supports both code-free and code-based data workflows, making it suitable for data engineers, developers, and architects across varying skill levels. Whether you're building ETL pipelines, ingesting real-time data, or performing data transformation using Spark or SQL, ADF provides a unified platform with deep integration across the Azure ecosystem.

This section covers the architecture, core concepts, activities, security features, pipeline design best practices, and integration patterns that make Azure Data Factory a critical component of scalable data engineering in the cloud.

---

### Architecture of Azure Data Factory

ADF IS BUILT UPON A set of cloud-native components designed to manage data movement and transformation across various environments:

- **Pipeline**: A logical grouping of activities that perform data tasks.
- **Activity**: A single step in a pipeline (e.g., copy data, execute SQL, run notebook).

- **Dataset**: Metadata about the data you're working with, pointing to tables, files, or directories.

- **Linked Service**: Connection string or credential reference to connect with source/target systems.

- **Integration Runtime (IR)**: Compute infrastructure used by ADF to perform actions (e.g., Azure-hosted, Self-hosted, or SSIS).

ADF provides more than 90 built-in connectors for Azure, on-premises, and third-party platforms, including SQL Server, Oracle, SAP, Amazon S3, Salesforce, and REST APIs.

---

## Core Concepts

### Pipelines and Activities

A **pipeline** in ADF is a container for one or more **activities**, which define the specific steps in the data workflow. These activities may include:

- **Copy Activity**: Move data from source to destination.

- **Data Flow Activity**: Transform data using a Spark-based visual editor.

- **Stored Procedure Activity**: Execute stored procedures in SQL databases.

- **Databricks Notebook Activity**: Run notebooks on an attached Databricks cluster.

- **Web and REST Activities**: Trigger external APIs.

- **Custom Activities**: Execute custom .NET code or scripts.

**Example JSON Structure of a Pipeline:**

```
{
"name": "Pipeline_ETL_SalesData",
"properties": {
"activities": [
{
"name": "CopySalesData",
"type": "Copy",
"inputs": [{ "referenceName": "SQLSalesSource", "type": "DatasetReference" }],
"outputs": [{ "referenceName": "BlobSalesTarget", "type": "DatasetReference" }],
"typeProperties": {
"source": { "type": "SqlSource" },
"sink": { "type": "BlobSink" }
}
}
]
}
}
```

**Datasets and Linked Services**

**DATASETS** define the structure and location of your data, including schema, file format, and folder path. They reference **Linked Services**, which contain the credentials and endpoint information for accessing the data.

**Example Linked Service** (SQL DB):

```
{
"name": "AzureSQLDB_LinkedService",
"type": "AzureSqlDatabase",
"typeProperties": {
"connectionString":
"Server=tcp:myserver.database.windows.net;Initial
Catalog=mydb;"
}
}
```

**Example Dataset** (CSV in Blob):

```
{
"name": "BlobSalesTarget",
"properties": {
"linkedServiceName": { "referenceName":
"BlobStorage_LinkedService", "type": "LinkedServiceReference" },
"type": "DelimitedText",
```

```
"typeProperties": {

"location": { "type": "AzureBlobStorageLocation", "fileName": "sales.csv", "folderPath": "cleansed/sales" },

"columnDelimiter": ",",

"firstRowAsHeader": true

}

}

}
```

---

## Integration Runtime (IR)

THE **Integration Runtime** (IR) is the compute infrastructure used to execute ADF pipeline activities. There are three types:

- **Azure IR**: Default runtime, used for cloud data movement and transformation.
- **Self-Hosted IR**: Installed on-premises or on VM for accessing local data sources.
- **Azure SSIS IR**: Allows lift-and-shift of existing SSIS packages to Azure.

**Self-hosted IR** is ideal when securely connecting to databases behind firewalls or when compliance prohibits cloud ingress.

**Example PowerShell Command to Create IR**:

```
New-AzDataFactoryV2IntegrationRuntimeSelfHosted `

-ResourceGroupName 'myResourceGroup' `
```

-DataFactoryName 'myDataFactory' `

-Name 'SelfHostedIR'

## Authoring and Deployment

ADF PROVIDES TWO PRIMARY ways to author pipelines:

- **Visual Studio Code / JSON**: Programmatic definition using ARM or JSON templates.
- **ADF Studio (Web UI)**: Drag-and-drop visual interface for building pipelines, managing triggers, and testing runs.

Deployment options include:

- **ARM Templates**
- **Azure DevOps CI/CD Pipelines**
- **Git Integration** for source control and collaboration

**Best Practices:**

- Use Git mode in ADF Studio to enable version control.
- Parameterize Linked Services and datasets for environment portability.
- Implement pipeline templates and modular design patterns.

## Data Flows: Spark-Based Transformations

**MAPPING DATA FLOWS** enable code-free transformations that run on managed Spark clusters. Operations include:

- Join, filter, aggregate, pivot, flatten

- Derived columns and data cleansing
- Surrogate key generation
- Schema drift handling

Data Flows are well suited for transformation in ELT scenarios, especially when targeting ADLS or Synapse.

**Example Transformation Flow:**

1. Source: Load from raw zone (CSV)
2. Derived Column: Normalize date format
3. Filter: Remove invalid records
4. Sink: Write to cleansed zone in Parquet

**Debug Mode** in Data Flows lets you preview transformations without full pipeline execution.

---

## Triggering Pipelines

ADF SUPPORTS SEVERAL triggering mechanisms:

- **Manual Trigger**: Run immediately via portal or API.
- **Schedule Trigger**: Execute on a defined interval (e.g., hourly, daily).
- **Event Trigger**: Respond to events like blob creation in ADLS.
- **Custom Trigger**: Use REST API or Azure Functions to start pipeline.

**Example: Event Trigger for ADLS File Arrival**

{

```
"type": "BlobEventsTrigger",
"typeProperties": {
"blobPathBeginsWith": "/raw/inventory/",
"events": ["Microsoft.Storage.BlobCreated"]
}
}
```

## Monitoring and Alerting

ADF INCLUDES RICH MONITORING capabilities for tracking pipeline executions, activity duration, data volumes, and failures.

- **ADF Monitor Tab**: View runs, filter by status, rerun failed pipelines.
- **Log Analytics Integration**: Centralize monitoring with other Azure services.
- **Alerts and Metrics**: Create custom alerts for pipeline failure or SLA violations.

**Log Analytics Kusto Example:**

```
ADFActivityRun
| where Status == "Failed"
| summarize count() by ActivityName, PipelineName, ErrorCode
```

**Alert Configuration:**

- Pipeline failure alerts via Azure Monitor

- Email, webhook, ITSM, or Azure Function as action

## Security and Access Control

ADF INTEGRATES WITH **Azure Active Directory (AAD)** and supports RBAC roles including:

- Data Factory Contributor
- Data Factory Operator
- Data Factory Reader

**Managed Identity** allows secure access to other Azure services without managing secrets.

**Key Vault Integration** enables storing secrets and using them in Linked Services:

```
"connectionString": {
"type": "AzureKeyVaultSecret",
"store": {
"referenceName": "MyKeyVault",
"type": "LinkedServiceReference"
},
"secretName": "SqlConnectionString"
}
```

## Common Pipeline Patterns

1. **Ingest from SQL → Transform → Load to ADLS**

  - ○ Use Copy Activity → Mapping Data Flow → Sink to Parquet

2. **Ingest from REST API → Store in Curated Zone**
   - ○ Use Web Activity → Copy Activity → Sink to ADLS
3. **Event-driven pipeline triggered by new file**
   - ○ Event Trigger → Schema validation → Enrich and write to curated zone
4. **Hybrid pattern using ADF + Databricks**
   - ○ ADF triggers Databricks notebook for complex ML transformations
5. **Incremental Load Pattern**
   - ○ Use watermark column or last-modified time filters
   - ○ Store state in Azure Table or SQL DB

---

## Summary

AZURE DATA FACTORY is a powerful and flexible service that forms the core of data movement and transformation in Azure-based architectures. By abstracting infrastructure concerns and providing a rich set of connectors and transformation options, ADF empowers data teams to build modular, scalable, and maintainable pipelines for batch and near-real-time processing. From traditional ETL workflows to modern ELT and event-driven paradigms, ADF integrates seamlessly with ADLS, Synapse, Databricks, and more, making it the go-to orchestration engine for Azure data engineering.

In the next section, we will explore how ADF pipelines integrate with **Azure Synapse** and **Azure Databricks**, enabling hybrid pipelines that span low-code, big data, and machine learning environments.

## Integrating with Azure Synapse and Databricks

IN MODERN DATA LAKE architectures on Azure, the orchestration and movement of data is only one part of the picture. The real value lies in the ability to process, analyze, and derive insights from data at scale. To support these advanced analytical workloads, two core services stand out in the Azure ecosystem—**Azure Synapse Analytics** and **Azure Databricks**. These platforms serve complementary roles and can be seamlessly integrated into data pipelines for advanced processing, big data transformation, SQL analytics, and machine learning.

This section will explore how Azure Data Factory (ADF), Azure Synapse, and Azure Databricks can be integrated to build powerful hybrid data pipelines. We will examine architectural patterns, integration techniques, use cases, code samples, and best practices for combining these tools to create an end-to-end analytics environment.

---

### Role of Synapse and Databricks in the Azure Data Landscape

WHILE BOTH SYNAPSE and Databricks are capable of processing large volumes of data, their strengths lie in different domains:

| Capability | Azure Synapse | Azure Databricks |
|---|---|---|
| SQL-based analysis | Strong (T-SQL engine) | Moderate (via Spark SQL) |
| Spark-based processing | Integrated Spark (limited control) | Fully managed Apache Spark |
| Machine Learning | Limited (via SynapseML) | Advanced ML (notebooks, MLflow) |
| Data Warehousing | Synapse Dedicated Pools | Not applicable |
| Batch ETL | Powerful with SQL/ ADF integration | Powerful with Delta + Spark |
| Real-time processing | Limited | Structured Streaming support |
| Notebooks and collaboration | Basic | Advanced (multi-user notebooks) |

They can both access Azure Data Lake Storage (ADLS), integrate with ADF, and use linked services for pipeline execution.

## Integrating Azure Synapse in Pipelines

### Use Cases

- SQL-BASED TRANSFORMATIONS of curated datasets
- Building star/snowflake schemas for BI
- Power BI semantic layer integration
- Serverless SQL access to raw files in ADLS

**Integration Methods**

1. **Synapse as a Sink/Source in ADF Pipelines**

    ○ ADF can ingest data into Synapse (Dedicated SQL Pools) using the Copy activity.

    ○ Can also extract data from Synapse into other sinks (e.g., ADLS, SQL).

2. **Stored Procedure Activity**

    ○ ADF pipelines can invoke stored procedures in Synapse for transformations.

3. **Serverless SQL Queries via ADF**

    ○ Lightweight ELT transformations using OPENROWSET with external tables.

4. **Notebooks in Synapse Studio**

    ○ Support for PySpark, Scala, .NET Spark for interactive exploration.

**Example ADF Activity: Load to Synapse Table**

```
{
"name": "LoadToSynapse",
"type": "Copy",
"typeProperties": {
"source": { "type": "DelimitedTextSource" },
```

```
"sink": {
"type": "SqlSink",
"preCopyScript": "TRUNCATE TABLE sales_fact;"
}
},
"inputs": [{ "referenceName": "CuratedSalesDataset", "type": "DatasetReference" }],
"outputs": [{ "referenceName": "SynapseSalesTable", "type": "DatasetReference" }]
}
```

**Serverless SQL Sample**

```
SELECT productId, SUM(quantity) AS total_quantity
FROM OPENROWSET(
BULK 'https://datalake.dfs.core.windows.net/curated/sales/*.parquet',
FORMAT='PARQUET'
) AS sales
GROUP BY productId;
```

**Best Practices**

- USE **dedicated SQL pools** for high-performance warehousing needs.

- Use **serverless SQL pools** for ad hoc and lightweight queries.
- Leverage **external tables and views** for abstraction and schema enforcement.
- Partition data in ADLS to optimize query performance.
- Monitor resource usage via Synapse Workspace metrics.

---

## Integrating Azure Databricks in Pipelines

### Use Cases

- COMPLEX TRANSFORMATIONS using PySpark or Scala
- Machine learning model development and scoring
- Delta Lake management with ACID transactions
- Handling schema evolution and semi-structured data
- Real-time streaming and event processing

### Integration Methods

1. **ADF → Databricks Notebook Activity**
    - Trigger Databricks notebooks directly from ADF pipelines.
2. **Databricks as Orchestrator**
    - Use Databricks Workflows or Jobs to coordinate transformations.
3. **Mounting ADLS in Databricks**

○ Use service principal or passthrough authentication to mount storage.

4. **Delta Lake Integration**

○ Use Delta format for reliable table management and time travel.

**Example ADF Notebook Activity**

```
{
"name": "RunDatabricksTransformation",
"type": "DatabricksNotebook",
"linkedServiceName": { "referenceName": "Databricks_LinkedService", "type": "LinkedServiceReference" },
"typeProperties": {
"notebookPath": "/Shared/TransformSalesData",
"baseParameters": {
"source_path": "raw/sales/",
"target_path": "curated/sales/"
}
}
}
```

**Sample Databricks Notebook Code (PySpark)**

df = spark.read.json(f"/mnt/datalake/{dbutils.widgets.get('source_path')}")

df_clean = df.filter("status = 'complete'").withColumn("revenue", df["quantity"] * df["unit_price"])

df_clean.write.format("delta").mode("overwrite").save(f"/mnt/datalake/{dbutils.widgets.get('target_path')}")

**Delta Lake Advantages**

- **ACID transactions** for reliable data updates and deletes.
- **Schema enforcement** to prevent bad data ingestion.
- **Time travel** to query historical data states.
- **Merge** support for upserts and slowly changing dimensions (SCD2).

**Example Merge Statement in Databricks**

MERGE INTO sales_curated AS target

USING updates AS source

ON target.order_id = source.order_id

WHEN MATCHED THEN UPDATE SET *

WHEN NOT MATCHED THEN INSERT *;

**Authentication and Access**

- **Service Principal with Secret Scope**: Store credentials securely and mount ADLS.

- **Azure Managed Identity**: Simpler and more secure access using RBAC.
- **Cluster policies**: Define resource limits and environment settings for users.

---

## Combined ADF + Synapse + Databricks Pattern

**SCENARIO**: Ingest sales data from on-premises SQL Server, transform in Databricks, store curated results in Synapse for Power BI reporting.

1. **ADF Copy Activity**
   - Extracts from SQL Server to ADLS /raw/sales/.
2. **ADF Databricks Notebook Activity**
   - Transforms raw sales data into Delta format at /curated/sales/.
3. **ADF Stored Procedure Activity**
   - Loads final aggregates into Synapse table dbo.sales_summary.
4. **Power BI**
   - Connects to Synapse Dedicated Pool and queries sales_summary.

**Benefits of this Hybrid Design**:

- Uses right tool for each task: ADF for orchestration, Databricks for Spark-based transformation, Synapse for BI-ready SQL analytics.

- Enables modular, scalable, and maintainable pipeline design.
- Enhances reusability of notebooks, views, and stored procedures.

## Monitoring and Observability

BOTH SYNAPSE AND DATABRICKS provide native monitoring features:

**Synapse:**

- Monitor hub for query execution and activity run history.
- Integration with Azure Log Analytics for detailed metrics.

**Databricks:**

- Job run logs and result visualizations.
- MLflow for experiment tracking and model lifecycle.
- Structured Streaming UI for monitoring streaming queries.

**ADF:**

- Pipeline runs show duration, row count, and error details.
- Alerting via Azure Monitor or email/webhook actions.

## Cost Management Considerations

- USE **serverless SQL** in Synapse for sporadic queries instead of provisioning dedicated pools.
- Use **Databricks Jobs Clusters** instead of all-purpose clusters to optimize costs.
- Monitor and auto-scale Spark clusters based on workload.

- Store intermediate files in cold storage tiers if not frequently accessed.

---

## Summary

AZURE SYNAPSE AND AZURE Databricks each bring distinct strengths to the Azure data platform. Synapse is ideal for SQL-based workloads, BI consumption, and warehousing, while Databricks excels in Spark-based processing, machine learning, and handling unstructured or semi-structured data. When integrated with Azure Data Factory, these services create a powerful trifecta that enables enterprises to ingest, transform, and analyze data at scale, with performance, reliability, and maintainability.

In the next section, we'll explore real-time data processing and how Azure Stream Analytics, Event Hubs, and Databricks Structured Streaming can be used to implement responsive and intelligent streaming data pipelines.

# Real-Time Processing with Azure Stream Analytics

IN THE ERA OF DIGITAL transformation, organizations are increasingly relying on real-time insights to power business-critical decisions. Whether it's monitoring financial transactions for fraud, analyzing telemetry from IoT devices, or generating live dashboards, the ability to process and act upon streaming data is now an essential capability of modern data platforms. Azure Stream Analytics (ASA), along with complementary services such as Azure Event Hubs, IoT Hub, and Azure Data Lake Storage, forms the backbone of Azure's real-time data processing ecosystem.

This section provides a comprehensive exploration of Azure Stream Analytics, covering architecture, key features, query language, integration patterns, deployment strategies, and best practices. We also explore how ASA can be used in conjunction with Azure Data Factory, Azure Synapse, and Databricks for hybrid streaming-batch scenarios.

---

## Understanding Streaming Data

STREAMING DATA IS GENERATED continuously by sources such as sensors, applications, logs, social media, and websites. It is characterized by its high volume, velocity, and variability, and is typically processed incrementally using stream processing engines.

**Key properties:**

- Data is unbounded and time-sensitive.
- Requires low-latency ingestion and transformation.
- May arrive out of order or with delay.
- Often processed using time windows and aggregation.

---

## Azure Stream Analytics Overview

AZURE STREAM ANALYTICS (ASA) is a serverless real-time analytics service designed to process streaming data from multiple sources simultaneously. It enables users to write simple SQL-like queries that operate over windows of streaming events and output results to various sinks.

**Core Features:**

- Serverless: No infrastructure management required.
- SQL-like query language with built-in temporal and analytical functions.

- Seamless integration with Event Hubs, IoT Hub, ADLS, Synapse, Power BI, and more.
- Scalable and highly available.
- Built-in support for windowing, joins, and user-defined functions (UDFs).

---

## ASA Architecture

A TYPICAL AZURE STREAM Analytics architecture consists of the following components:

1. **Input**: Data from Event Hubs, IoT Hub, or Blob Storage.
2. **Query**: SQL-based transformation logic applied to incoming streams.
3. **Output**: Transformed data is sent to sinks such as ADLS, Synapse, Power BI, Azure Functions, or SQL Database.

**Example Architecture Flow:**

- Devices → Azure IoT Hub → Azure Stream Analytics → ADLS (curated zone)
- Applications → Event Hubs → ASA → Power BI Dashboard
- Event Logs → Blob Storage → ASA → Synapse for analysis

---

## Stream Analytics Query Language

ASA QUERIES ARE DEFINED using a subset of T-SQL extended with temporal logic. Queries are evaluated over sliding or tumbling windows, allowing for real-time aggregation and filtering.

**Example Query: Tumbling Window Aggregation**

SELECT

deviceId,

AVG(temperature) AS avg_temp,

System.Timestamp AS window_end

INTO

curated.iot_5min_avg

FROM

iot_stream TIMESTAMP BY eventTime

GROUP BY

TumblingWindow(minute, 5), deviceId

**Key Concepts:**

- **TIMESTAMP BY**: Defines the event time for windowing.
- **TumblingWindow**: Fixed-size, non-overlapping windows.
- **HoppingWindow**: Fixed-size, overlapping windows.
- **SlidingWindow**: Continuously updating window based on event time.
- **SessionWindow**: Grouping of events separated by gaps of inactivity.

**Join Example: Enriching Event Stream**

SELECT

s.deviceId,

```
s.reading,
m.deviceType
INTO
enriched_stream
FROM
sensor_stream s
JOIN
metadata_table m
ON
s.deviceId = m.deviceId
```

**User-Defined Functions (UDFs):**

Stream Analytics supports JavaScript UDFs for custom logic:

```
function main(input) {
return input.toUpperCase();
}
```

---

## Input and Output Integration

**Supported Inputs:**

- **Azure Event Hubs**: High-throughput ingestion for app and device telemetry.
- **Azure IoT Hub**: Purpose-built for IoT scenarios.

- **Azure Blob Storage**: Supports batch or replay of historical data.
- **Azure Data Lake Storage**: Used for archived log reprocessing.

**Supported Outputs:**

- **Azure Data Lake Storage Gen2**: Append-mode or partitioned write.
- **Azure SQL Database**: Real-time updates into operational stores.
- **Azure Synapse Analytics**: Streaming data warehouse use cases.
- **Power BI**: Direct integration for live dashboards.
- **Azure Functions**: Trigger downstream workflows or ML scoring.
- **Event Hubs**: Forward data to other consumers.

**Example Output to ADLS:**

```
{
"type": "DataLakeStorageV2",
"properties": {
"accountName": "mystorageaccount",
"filePathPrefix": "iot/curated/{date}/{time}",
"dateFormat": "yyyy/MM/dd",
"timeFormat": "HH"
}
}
```

## Windowing and Temporal Analysis

REAL-TIME PROCESSING relies heavily on **window functions** for aggregating and analyzing time-series data. Azure Stream Analytics supports:

- **Tumbling Windows**: Non-overlapping, fixed duration.
- **Hopping Windows**: Fixed duration, overlapping intervals.
- **Sliding Windows**: Event-driven updates.
- **Session Windows**: Inactivity-based grouping.

**Example: Hopping Window**

```
SELECT

COUNT(*) AS message_count,

System.Timestamp AS window_end

INTO

event_counts

FROM

event_stream TIMESTAMP BY enqueuedTime

GROUP BY

HoppingWindow(minute, 10, 5)
```

**Use Case Examples:**

- Calculate moving averages of temperature sensors.
- Track active users in rolling 15-minute windows.

- Detect spikes in error logs within 3-minute intervals.

## Monitoring and Debugging

ASA PROVIDES RICH TELEMETRY and diagnostics through:

- **Job metrics**: Input rate, output rate, watermark delay, and function calls.
- **Diagnostic logs**: Enabled via Azure Monitor and Log Analytics.
- **Alerts**: Triggered based on query failures or latency issues.
- **Preview data**: Test inputs and outputs interactively before publishing.

**Common Metrics to Watch:**

- Late arrival rate
- Out-of-order events
- Deserialization errors
- Input and output throughput
- Job backpressure and checkpoint delay

## Scalability and Performance

- **Streaming Units (SUs)**: Measure of compute, memory, and throughput allocated to a job.
- Each SU supports approx. 1 MB/s input and 3 MB/s output throughput.
- Scale out by increasing SUs or partitioning input streams.

**Performance Tuning Tips:**

- Use partitioned inputs and outputs where possible.
- Use WHERE clauses to filter early.
- Avoid unnecessary joins or complex UDFs.
- Aggregate at the edge (IoT Edge) when feasible.

**Auto-Scaling:**

While ASA does not auto-scale automatically, you can use Azure Monitor metrics to trigger Logic Apps or Functions that adjust SUs dynamically using ARM templates or PowerShell scripts.

---

## Hybrid Pipeline Design: Batch + Stream

REAL-WORLD SYSTEMS often require a blend of batch and streaming processing. ASA can be integrated with Azure Data Factory or Synapse Pipelines to enable hybrid workflows:

**Pattern Example:**

1. **Stream ingestion**: ASA processes incoming sensor data.
2. **Store curated stream**: Output to ADLS as hourly parquet files.
3. **Daily aggregation**: ADF batch pipeline summarizes hourly files into daily report.
4. **Serve**: Final results loaded into Synapse or visualized in Power BI.

This pattern provides:

- Real-time responsiveness for alerts and monitoring.

- Batch-based precision and reprocessing.
- Storage cost optimization via tiered processing.

---

## Security and Compliance

- **Role-Based Access Control (RBAC)** for managing job access.
- **Managed Identity** for secure access to ADLS and Event Hubs.
- **Network Isolation** via VNet integration (Private Link supported).
- **Data Encryption** in transit (TLS 1.2) and at rest.
- **Compliance Certifications**: HIPAA, GDPR, ISO, SOC, and more.

**Key Vault Integration:**

Use Key Vault to manage secrets for Event Hub SAS keys or ADLS credentials in job configuration.

---

## Summary

AZURE STREAM ANALYTICS enables real-time data processing that is scalable, declarative, and deeply integrated with the Azure ecosystem. By offering a familiar SQL-based interface, it allows rapid development of powerful streaming pipelines that can react to events, transform data on the fly, and drive actionable insights within seconds. Whether powering IoT dashboards, triggering alerts, or feeding ML inference pipelines, ASA provides the infrastructure and flexibility to handle time-sensitive data workloads at scale.

In the next chapter, we move into performance engineering and data pipeline optimization, where we will explore partitioning, indexing, metadata management, and cost controls to ensure your data architecture remains robust and scalable as it grows.

# Chapter 4: Designing for Performance and Scale

## Partitioning Strategies in ADLS

PARTITIONING IS A FUNDAMENTAL design principle in building scalable and performant data lake architectures. As data volumes grow and analytics workloads become increasingly complex, effective partitioning ensures that queries are optimized, storage remains manageable, and data pipelines run efficiently. In Azure Data Lake Storage (ADLS), partitioning plays a critical role in enabling high-performance reads, supporting schema-on-read architectures, reducing scan sizes, and improving cost efficiency.

This section explores the theory, practices, and real-world applications of partitioning strategies in ADLS. We will cover partitioning fundamentals, naming conventions, tools and formats, partition pruning, and how these strategies interact with Azure Synapse, Databricks, and serverless compute services. Code snippets and examples will also be included to demonstrate implementation techniques.

---

### What is Partitioning?

PARTITIONING IS THE process of dividing large datasets into smaller, more manageable segments based on specific keys or criteria—typically time, geography, status, or category. In a data lake, this is implemented using **folder-level structure**, where each partition is represented by a subdirectory in the file system.

**Example Folder Structure:**

/sales/year=2024/month=01/day=01/

/sales/year=2024/month=01/day=02/

/logs/region=us/state=tx/day=2025-05-01/

/events/event_type=login/year=2025/month=04/

Partitioning enables:

- Faster queries by scanning only relevant partitions.
- Better organization and lifecycle management of data.
- Parallel processing by distributed engines like Spark and Synapse.

## Why Partitioning Matters

IN BIG DATA ENVIRONMENTS, improper data layout can lead to:

- Long query times due to full directory scans.
- High storage and compute costs.
- Poor user experience in downstream analytics.

Partitioning improves:

- **Query performance** through predicate pushdown.
- **Pipeline scalability** by enabling parallelism.
- **Data management** via targeted retention policies and archiving.
- **Cost efficiency** by reducing compute time.

## Common Partitioning Strategies

### 1. Time-Based Partitioning

THIS IS THE MOST COMMON and natural form of partitioning for event, log, and transactional data.

**Folder Convention:**

/dataset/year=2025/month=05/day=12/

/dataset/ingestion_date=2025-05-12/

**Best For:**

- IoT telemetry
- Web logs
- Financial transactions

**Benefits:**

- Supports time-windowed queries and retention.
- Aligns with pipeline schedules (daily/hourly runs).
- Compatible with Azure Monitor, Stream Analytics, and Databricks.

### 2. Category-Based Partitioning

PARTITIONING BY DOMAIN-specific attributes.

**Example:**

/customers/region=emea/

/products/category=electronics/

/support/ticket_status=resolved/

**Best For:**

- Datasets where queries filter by category or label.
- Serving dashboards or ML models segmented by business criteria.

**Considerations:**

- Ensure partition cardinality (distinct values) is reasonable.
- Avoid high-cardinality attributes like UUIDs or emails.

### 3. Composite Partitioning

COMBINING TIME AND category-based partitioning.

**Example:**

/sales/region=na/year=2025/month=05/day=12/

/logs/level=error/year=2025/month=05/

**Use Cases:**

- Optimizing for both reporting and lifecycle management.
- Supporting multi-dimensional queries in OLAP-like scenarios.

**Warning:**

- Too many levels or attributes may increase folder complexity.

## Partition Pruning and Pushdown

PARTITION PRUNING REFERS to the ability of query engines to skip non-relevant partitions during execution. For this to work:

- Partition columns must be used in the query filter.
- Folder structure must match the partition definition.
- Engines must support pushdown for the file format (e.g., Parquet, Delta).

**Databricks Example:**

```
df = spark.read.option("basePath", "/mnt/datalake/sales/").parquet("/mnt/datalake/sales/year=2025/month=05/")

df_filtered = df.filter("day = '12' AND region = 'us'")
```

**Synapse Serverless SQL Example:**

```
SELECT *

FROM OPENROWSET(

BULK 'https://mystorageaccount.dfs.core.windows.net/sales/year=2025/month=05/*.parquet',

FORMAT='PARQUET'

) WITH (

region VARCHAR(10),

amount FLOAT

) AS sales

WHERE region = 'us';
```

**Key Formats That Support Pruning:**

- Parquet (Columnar, highly optimized)
- Delta Lake (with transaction log)
- ORC

CSV and JSON do **not** support predicate pushdown efficiently.

## Tools and Services for Partitioning

### Azure Data Factory (ADF)

- PARTITION FOLDERS can be parameterized in dataset definitions.
- Supports dynamic path resolution based on pipeline variables.

**Example:**

```
"path": {
"value": "sales/year=@{formatDateTime(pipeline().TriggerTime, 'yyyy')}/month=@{formatDateTime(pipeline().TriggerTime, 'MM')}/",
"type": "Expression"
}
```

### Azure Databricks

- AUTO-DETECTS PARTITIONS when using .partitionBy() in write operations.

- Supports dynamic partition overwrite and Delta merge.

**Example:**

df.write.format("delta").partitionBy("year", "month", "day").mode("overwrite").save("/mnt/datalake/sales/")

**Azure Synapse Analytics**

- SUPPORTS PARTITIONING via external table definitions.
- Requires file path and structure to match partition schema.

**Best Practice:**

- Define external table partitioned by folder structure:

```
CREATE EXTERNAL TABLE sales_partitioned (
order_id INT,
region VARCHAR(50),
amount FLOAT
)
WITH (
LOCATION = 'sales/',
DATA_SOURCE = my_datalake,
FILE_FORMAT = my_parquet_format
)
```

## Partition Granularity and File Size Considerations

### GRANULARITY TRADEOFFS:

- **Fine-Grained (hour/day)**:
  - Pros: Enables precise queries, better lifecycle control.
  - Cons: Risk of many small files (file system overhead).
- **Coarse-Grained (month/region)**:
  - Pros: Fewer files, simpler structure.
  - Cons: Slower queries for filtered scenarios.

**File Size Recommendations:**

- Target 100 MB to 1 GB per file.
- Avoid creating many small files ("small files problem").
- Use repartitioning or coalescing techniques in Databricks:

```
df.repartition(10).write.parquet("/path/")
```

## Data Lifecycle and Partition-Based Management

PARTITIONING SIMPLIFIES:

- **Retention policies**: Delete older partitions based on timestamp.
- **Archiving**: Move cold partitions to Cool or Archive tiers.
- **Auditability**: Trace lineage from raw to curated zones.

**ADF Custom Activity for Retention:**

az storage fs file delete-batch—account-name mystorage—file-system curated—pattern "year=2023/*"

**Lifecycle Policy Example:**

```
{
"rules": [
{
"enabled": true,
"name": "cold-data",
"definition": {
"filters": {
"blobTypes": ["blockBlob"],
"prefixMatch": ["sales/year=2022/"]
},
"actions": {
"baseBlob": {
"tierToCool": { "daysAfterModificationGreaterThan": 30 },
"delete": { "daysAfterModificationGreaterThan": 180 }
}
}
}
}
```

```
]
}
```

## Best Practices

- DESIGN PARTITION strategy before ingestion starts.
- Match partition columns to high-frequency query filters.
- Use columnar formats (Parquet, Delta) for efficient scans.
- Avoid high-cardinality partition keys.
- Monitor file count and partition sizes regularly.
- Automate partition pruning with external tools or table definitions.
- Use versioned paths (e.g., v1/, v2/) for schema evolution without breaking dependencies.

## Summary

PARTITIONING IS NOT a mere storage technique—it's a performance engineering discipline. In Azure Data Lake architectures, effective partitioning can dramatically improve query performance, optimize compute costs, and simplify pipeline orchestration. By aligning your folder structures, file formats, and data flow design with a solid partitioning strategy, you unlock the full power of scalable analytics on Azure.

As we move forward, the next section will dive into how you can further optimize pipeline execution through caching, transformations, pipeline orchestration, and concurrency management to build truly performant cloud-native data systems.

# Optimizing Pipeline Performance

PERFORMANCE OPTIMIZATION is a critical aspect of building resilient, cost-effective, and scalable data pipelines. As data volumes increase and use cases expand to include real-time processing, machine learning, and complex transformations, even the most well-designed pipelines can encounter latency bottlenecks, resource overuse, and concurrency limits. In Azure, where cloud-native pipelines are typically built with Azure Data Factory (ADF), Azure Synapse Analytics, Databricks, and Azure Stream Analytics, ensuring optimal performance requires a combination of architectural choices, implementation strategies, and continuous monitoring.

This section provides a deep dive into performance optimization techniques across the entire data pipeline lifecycle—from ingestion and transformation to storage and consumption. Topics covered include data size management, parallelism, file format choices, transformation tuning, integration runtime scaling, caching strategies, and execution plan analysis.

---

## Performance Bottlenecks in Data Pipelines

UNDERSTANDING WHERE performance degradation occurs is key to applying the right optimization strategies. Common bottlenecks include:

- **Slow data sources** (e.g., APIs, legacy RDBMS)
- **Small files or inefficient partitioning**
- **Suboptimal data formats**
- **Overloaded or underpowered integration runtimes**

- **Inefficient transformations or joins**
- **Cold-start latencies in Spark jobs**
- **Lack of predicate pushdown or data skipping**

Performance tuning is a multi-dimensional effort, requiring attention to storage layout, transformation logic, and runtime execution.

---

## Optimizing Data Ingestion

### Parallel Reads and Copy Activity

IN AZURE DATA FACTORY, **Copy Activity** can be optimized using parallelism, staging, and throughput settings.

**Techniques:**

- Enable **parallel copy** by partitioning source data using ranges or columns (e.g., date ranges, ID buckets).
- Use **polybase** or **staged copy** for large-scale loads into Synapse.
- Choose **binary copy** for performance when schema inference is not needed.
- Tune **data integration units (DIUs)** in Self-Hosted IRs for throughput-sensitive operations.

**Example: Configuring Parallelism**

"translator": {

"type": "TabularTranslator",

"typeProperties": {

"columnMappings": {

"source_col": "target_col"

}

}

},

"parallelCopies": 8

**Best Practice:**

- Avoid single-threaded ingest unless absolutely required.
- Split ingestion tasks by time or ID range for better concurrency.

**Source Optimization**

FOR RELATIONAL DATABASES:

- Use **indexed columns** in WHERE clauses.
- Retrieve only required columns (no SELECT * queries).
- Offload filtering and joins to the database when possible.

For REST APIs:

- Use pagination.
- Reduce payload size by selecting only needed fields.
- Apply server-side filters when available.

## Transformation Optimization

### Data Flow Tuning in Azure Data Factory

ADF'S MAPPING DATA Flows are executed on Apache Spark under the hood. Performance depends heavily on how operations are written and ordered.

**Optimization Tips:**

- Use **broadcast joins** for small dimension tables.
- Cache reused datasets with the cache() transformation.
- Use **filter and select** early to reduce data volume in pipeline.
- Avoid unneeded **Derived Column** transformations that increase memory pressure.
- Inspect the **Data Flow Debug Execution Plan** for bottlenecks.

**Example: Using Broadcast Join**

```
"transformation": {
"type": "Join",
"typeProperties": {
"broadcast": true,
"joinType": "inner",
"leftJoinKey": "customer_id",
"rightJoinKey": "id"
}
```

}

**Best Practice:**

- Use **sink partitioning** to balance writes.
- Prefer **Delta** or **Parquet** as sink format to enable vectorized reads later.

## Spark Optimization in Databricks

DATABRICKS OFFERS DEEP tuning capabilities via Spark's configuration parameters.

**Key Techniques:**

- Cache intermediate datasets (df.cache())
- Use **coalesce()** to reduce number of small files.
- Avoid shuffling with partition-aware operations.
- Leverage **Adaptive Query Execution (AQE)** for dynamic join and shuffle strategy selection.
- Persist large joins if reused across stages.

**Example:**

```
df = spark.read.parquet("/mnt/raw/orders/")

df_clean = df.filter(df["status"] == "delivered").cache()

df_clean.write.mode("overwrite").parquet("/mnt/curated/orders/")
```

## Storage and Format Optimization

### Choosing Efficient File Formats

COLUMNAR FORMATS SIGNIFICANTLY improve read performance for analytics:

| Format | Characteristics | Best For |
|---|---|---|
| CSV | Human-readable, but slow and large | Compatibility scenarios |
| JSON | Flexible schema, inefficient storage | Nested data, APIs |
| Parquet | Columnar, compressed, fast reads | Analytics, Synapse, Spark |
| Delta | Parquet + ACID + time travel | ML pipelines, real-time pipelines |
| Avro | Schema evolution, row-based | Serialization use cases |

**Best Practice:**

- Use **Parquet or Delta** for all transformed or curated data.
- Avoid small CSV files; coalesce or repartition before writing.

### Partitioning

PARTITIONING ALLOWS for **predicate pushdown** and **file skipping**.

**Strategies:**

- Time-based: /year=2024/month=01/
- Category-based: /region=us/

Combine with **Parquet** or **Delta** for best performance.

---

## Runtime and Compute Optimization

### Integration Runtimes in ADF

CHOOSE THE CORRECT **IR** type:

- **Azure IR**: Cloud-based, scales automatically.
- **Self-hosted IR**: Best for on-prem or VNet-secured resources.
- **SSIS IR**: For migrating legacy SSIS packages.

**Optimization Parameters:**

- Set **concurrency limits** to avoid IR overload.
- Use **scaling rules** to allocate more DIUs for large workloads.

**Monitoring Tooling:**

- ADF Monitoring dashboard
- Azure Monitor and Log Analytics integration

### Spark Clusters in Databricks

- USE **Job Clusters** for one-off workloads to reduce cost.
- Enable **autoscaling** to dynamically adjust worker count.
- Profile jobs using **Spark UI** and **Event Logs**.

**Cluster Sizing Guide:**

- 8–16 cores for medium pipelines

- Enable **photon runtime** for performance boost (SQL workloads)
- Use **DBIO metrics** to profile read performance

## Caching and Reuse

CACHING INTERMEDIATE results improves performance when:

- The dataset is reused multiple times.
- The data is too expensive to recompute.

**ADF Data Flow Cache Example:**

```
{
"type": "Cache",
"name": "CachedCustomerData",
"cacheType": "Memory"
}
```

**Databricks Example:**

```
customer_df.cache()
```

**Use Cases:**

- Enriched dimensions reused across joins.
- Pre-aggregated facts in a star schema.

## Monitoring and Diagnostics

USE BUILT-IN AND INTEGRATED tools for proactive performance management:

- **ADF Monitoring**: Activity run time, throughput, errors.
- **Databricks Jobs UI**: DAG visualization, Spark stage metrics.
- **Synapse Monitoring**: Query plans, execution stats.
- **Azure Monitor**: Log metrics, thresholds, alerts.
- **Log Analytics**: Custom dashboards and Kusto queries.

**Log Analytics Example:**

ADFActivityRun

| where Status == "Failed"

| summarize failures = count() by ActivityName

**Key Metrics:**

- Rows processed per minute
- Job duration and cost
- Pipeline throughput
- Retry count and error codes

---

## Best Practices Checklist

- ◈ CHOOSE COLUMNAR formats for analytics workloads.
- ◈ Partition data based on query access patterns.

- � Use caching for frequently reused datasets.
- � Prune and coalesce small files during batch writes.
- � Limit data transformation steps to essentials.
- � Allocate sufficient DIUs or cluster nodes.
- � Tune parallelism and data shuffling in Spark.
- � Monitor and alert on job duration and error frequency.
- � Implement back-pressure controls in streaming pipelines.
- � Optimize joins (broadcast small, avoid cartesian).

### Summary

PIPELINE PERFORMANCE optimization is a continuous and essential process in cloud-scale data systems. From the careful selection of data formats and partitioning strategies to the fine-tuning of transformation logic and compute environments, every decision impacts latency, cost, and scalability. Azure's tools provide powerful capabilities—but must be combined with best practices, performance profiling, and architectural rigor to yield optimal results.

In the next section, we will explore metadata management and how tools like Azure Purview can help you enforce governance, enable lineage tracking, and support compliant, scalable metadata-driven pipeline operations.

## Managing Metadata with Azure Purview

IN MODERN CLOUD DATA architectures, the volume and complexity of data assets can quickly overwhelm traditional cataloging methods. As organizations adopt data lakes, data warehouses, SaaS applications, and hybrid environments, they face a growing challenge: how to manage metadata—data about the data—in a centralized, scalable, and intelligent way. Metadata is not simply an afterthought; it is foundational for governance, discovery, lineage tracking, privacy enforcement, and analytics acceleration. Azure Purview (now part of Microsoft Purview) addresses this challenge by offering a unified data governance service to catalog, classify, manage, and monitor enterprise data across on-premises, multicloud, and SaaS environments.

This section explores the role of metadata in Azure-based data platforms, provides a detailed overview of Azure Purview's architecture and capabilities, and presents practical guidance for implementing a metadata-driven ecosystem. It includes real-world use cases, schema and classification strategies, data lineage capture, and integration with other Azure services like Synapse, ADF, and Power BI.

---

## What is Metadata?

**METADATA** is descriptive information that provides context and structure to data. It helps users understand the meaning, lineage, usage, and sensitivity of data assets.

**Types of Metadata:**

1. **Technical Metadata**
    - Schema, data types, file formats
    - Storage locations, table definitions, partitions
2. **Business Metadata**

  - Business glossary terms
  - Definitions, data owners, usage descriptions

3. **Operational Metadata**
  - Data freshness, access logs, run durations
  - ETL job status, success/failure logs

4. **Process Metadata**
  - Lineage, transformation logic
  - Dependency graphs and processing history

5. **Security Metadata**
  - Classification (e.g., PII, PHI)
  - Access control lists (ACLs), sensitivity labels

---

## The Role of Metadata in Data Lakes

DATA LAKES, BY DESIGN, are schema-agnostic, flexible, and scalable. However, without metadata, they risk becoming unmanageable **data swamps**. Metadata enables:

- **Data discovery**: Users can search and filter assets.
- **Trust and transparency**: Know where data came from and how it has been used.
- **Compliance**: Apply policies for GDPR, HIPAA, etc.

- **Automation**: Dynamically route and transform data based on schema or classification.

For Azure-native workloads, Microsoft Purview serves as the metadata backbone across ADLS, Synapse, Power BI, SQL Server, and beyond.

---

## Microsoft Purview Overview

MICROSOFT PURVIEW IS a unified governance service designed to manage and oversee the metadata and usage of data assets across your data estate.

**Key Capabilities:**

- **Data Catalog**: Centralized repository for all metadata assets.
- **Automated Scanning**: Connectors to over 20 sources including ADLS, Azure SQL, Synapse, and AWS S3.
- **Data Classification**: Built-in and custom classifiers (e.g., credit card, national ID).
- **Lineage Tracking**: Visual end-to-end flow of data from source to consumption.
- **Business Glossary**: Define and enforce common terminology across domains.
- **Role-Based Access Control**: Assign responsibilities for stewardship, classification, and curation.

---

## Architecture and Components

1. **Purview Account**

Core resource deployed into Azure; includes scanning, classification, and catalog capabilities.

2. **Data Map**
   Scalable, cloud-native graph that stores metadata, classification tags, lineage, and annotations.
3. **Scan Rulesets and Scans**
   Define how and when to crawl data sources for schema and metadata.
4. **Classification Engine**
   Uses pattern matching and ML to tag sensitive fields.
5. **Data Catalog Portal**
   UI for exploring assets, viewing lineage, applying glossary terms.
6. **Integration Connectors**
   Built-in connectors for Azure SQL, Synapse, ADLS, Power BI, Amazon S3, SAP, and more.

---

## Setting Up Azure Purview

**STEP 1**: Create a Purview account.

```
az purview account create \

—name myPurview \

—resource-group myRG \

—location eastus \

—sku Standard
```

**Step 2**: Assign permissions (Reader, Curator, Data Source Admin).

**Step 3**: Register data sources like ADLS Gen2, Synapse, SQL DB.

**Step 4**: Define scan rules (schedule, file types, classification).

**Step 5**: Run initial scan and review discovered assets.

## Metadata Scanning in Practice

**SCANNING ADLS GEN2**:

- Register the storage account.
- Set scan scope to specific containers or folders.
- Enable classification of files: CSV, Parquet, JSON, etc.

**Supported Formats**:

- Structured: SQL Tables, Parquet, Delta, CSV
- Semi-structured: JSON, Avro
- Unstructured: Office docs, PDFs (metadata only)

**Scheduling Options**:

- One-time, daily, weekly scans
- Use incremental scans to limit cost and compute usage

## Data Classification

PURVIEW INCLUDES 100+ built-in classifiers to automatically identify data types, including:

- Personal Identifiable Information (PII)
- Financial (credit cards, account numbers)
- Health (ICD-10 codes, prescriptions)

- Confidential or internal documents

**Custom Classifiers**:

- Regex-based or ML-based
- Apply to specific columns or fields in structured sources

**Example: Tagging PII in ADLS Parquet File**

- Classifier matches patterns like email, SSN, phone number
- Automatically tags customer_email as PII

## Business Glossary and Domains

A ROBUST GLOSSARY ENSURES data is consistently understood across the organization.

**Glossary Features**:

- Term definitions with examples
- Term relationships (synonyms, children, parents)
- Steward assignment and curation workflow

**Domains**:

- Group related assets and glossary terms by business unit (e.g., Finance, Sales, HR)

**Usage Example**:

- Link glossary term "Customer ID" to field cust_id in 18 datasets across SQL and ADLS.

## Lineage and Impact Analysis

PURVIEW AUTOMATICALLY captures **lineage** for data pipelines when integrated with:

- **Azure Data Factory**
- **Azure Synapse Pipelines**
- **Power BI Datasets**
- **Azure SQL stored procedures**

**Lineage Graph Capabilities**:

- Trace data from source to final report
- Identify dependencies and upstream/downstream impact
- Support change management (who/what will be affected)

**Example Use Case**:

- A product manager can trace a KPI in Power BI back to the SQL stored procedure and the original ADLS file.

---

## Integration with Azure Services

### Azure Synapse Analytics

- DISCOVER PURVIEW-registered datasets directly in Synapse Studio.
- Attach metadata and glossary terms to external tables.

**Azure Data Factory**

- AUTOMATICALLY SEND pipeline lineage to Purview.
- Show which datasets were read or written by which pipelines.

**Power BI**

- SCAN AND CLASSIFY Power BI datasets and lineage.
- View which dashboards are consuming a given dataset.

**Azure Monitor + Azure Policy**

- CREATE COMPLIANCE dashboards.
- Enforce policies (e.g., all PII-tagged assets must reside in encrypted storage).

---

## Best Practices for Metadata Management

- **Start with scanning critical data sources**: prioritize curated zones and SQL systems.
- **Automate scans** to maintain updated metadata.
- **Assign stewards and ownership** to ensure metadata quality.
- **Tag sensitive fields** for security and compliance.
- **Use glossary terms liberally** to drive consistency across teams.
- **Visualize lineage** before making changes to pipelines or schemas.
- **Integrate with CI/CD** to validate metadata as part of pipeline deployments.

---

## Use Case Scenarios

1. **Regulatory Compliance (GDPR, HIPAA)**

    ○ Automatically detect and catalog sensitive data.

    ○ Produce lineage reports for audit readiness.

2. **Self-Service Analytics**

    ○ Empower business users to find trusted datasets.

    ○ Reduce bottlenecks in data engineering teams.

3. **Data Quality Monitoring**

    ○ Track completeness, freshness, and modification history.

    ○ Flag stale or deprecated datasets.

4. **Cross-System Impact Analysis**

    ○ Trace changes in ADF pipelines that may affect Power BI dashboards.

    ○ Plan schema evolution with confidence.

---

## Summary

METADATA MANAGEMENT is not optional in a modern data platform—it is foundational. With Azure Purview, Microsoft offers a comprehensive solution for automating discovery, enforcing governance, managing classification, and surfacing lineage across the enterprise. By embedding Purview into the heart of your Azure architecture, you can unlock trusted, compliant, and discoverable data products at scale.

In the next section, we will explore how to monitor performance and cost across pipelines, storage, and compute services, ensuring operational excellence and continuous improvement across your data infrastructure.

# Performance Monitoring and Cost Management

AS CLOUD-BASED DATA platforms grow in complexity and scale, maintaining system performance while managing operational costs becomes a strategic imperative. Even well-architected data lakes and pipelines can incur escalating expenses or performance degradation if not continuously monitored and optimized. Azure provides a rich ecosystem of tools and telemetry to monitor the health, efficiency, and cost of every component in your data architecture—from storage and compute to orchestration and security. This section offers a detailed exploration of best practices, tools, and architectural strategies for performance monitoring and cost control in Azure Data Lake environments.

We will focus on practical techniques using Azure Monitor, Log Analytics, Azure Cost Management, metrics and alerts, integration with ADF, Synapse, Databricks, and ADLS, and governance mechanisms to enforce cost-effective practices across teams.

## Why Monitoring and Cost Management Matter

IN A DATA-DRIVEN ENTERPRISE, performance issues or uncontrolled cost growth can have broad implications:

- **Business Risk**: Delayed insights or unresponsive pipelines disrupt operations.
- **User Experience**: Slow dashboards or incomplete data reduce trust and usability.
- **Budget Constraints**: Unmonitored resources quickly exceed allocated budgets.
- **Compliance**: Non-adherence to performance SLAs or budget policies introduces compliance risks.

Proper monitoring ensures early detection of bottlenecks, while cost management enforces fiscal discipline without compromising innovation.

---

## Key Metrics to Track Across Azure Data Architecture

### Compute Metrics

- CPU AND MEMORY USAGE
- Execution duration and throughput
- Number of concurrent runs (pipelines, queries, jobs)
- Cold-start latency in Spark clusters

### Storage Metrics

- DATA READ/WRITE latency
- File size and object count
- Egress volume and access frequency

- Lifecycle policy effectiveness

**Pipeline Metrics**

- ACTIVITY RUN DURATION
- Success/failure count
- Data volumes moved
- Bottlenecks in sequential steps

**Cost Metrics**

- DAILY AND MONTHLY spend by service/resource group
- Cost anomalies or spikes
- Per-pipeline or per-dataset cost attribution
- Storage tier utilization and transitions

---

## Azure Monitor and Log Analytics

**AZURE MONITOR** is the unified service for collecting, analyzing, and acting on telemetry from Azure resources.

**Log Analytics** is the query engine behind Azure Monitor, using the powerful **Kusto Query Language (KQL)**.

**Key Monitoring Scenarios:**

- OBSERVE ADF PIPELINE executions in near real time.
- Monitor Databricks cluster performance and job statistics.

- Analyze ADLS access patterns and optimize storage tiering.
- Track query execution plans and duration in Synapse.

**Sample KQL Queries**

**PIPELINE FAILURES (ADF):**

```
ADFActivityRun
| where Status == "Failed"
| summarize failures = count() by PipelineName, ActivityName
```

**Databricks Job Duration:**

```
AzureDiagnostics
| where ResourceType == "databricks" and Category == "SparkListenerEvent"
| summarize avg(durationMs) by jobId
```

**Storage Access Patterns:**

```
StorageBlobLogs
| summarize readOps = count() by blobType, TimeGenerated
| order by TimeGenerated desc
```

## Cost Management Tools in Azure

AZURE OFFERS NATIVE tools to visualize, analyze, and forecast spend:

**Azure Cost Management + Billing**

- VISUALIZE SPENDING by resource, service, tag, or department.
- Set budgets and spending thresholds.
- Forecast future spending based on trends.
- Allocate cost using tags (e.g., "Project=ML", "Team=Finance").

**Cost Analysis Scenarios:**

- IDENTIFY TOP 10 most expensive pipelines or resources.
- Detect services with low utilization but high spend.
- Determine cost per dataset ingestion.
- Monitor storage tier distribution (Hot vs Cool vs Archive).

**Example Tagging Strategy:**

- Environment = prod|dev|test
- Pipeline = ingest_sales|ml_train
- Owner = alice@company.com

Apply via ARM templates or CLI:

```
az resource tag—tags Environment=prod Owner=alice@company.com—name mySynapseSQLPool—resource-group myRG
```

## Service-Specific Monitoring and Cost Control

### Azure Data Factory

- USE **ADF Monitor** for run history and performance breakdowns.
- Store logs in Log Analytics workspace for KQL-based analysis.
- Scale Integration Runtimes (IRs) appropriately based on pipeline concurrency.
- Use **cached datasets** and minimize unnecessary transformations.

**Cost Optimization Tips:**

- Use DIUs (Data Integration Units) sparingly.
- Avoid nested or redundant Copy Activities.
- Prefer parameterized datasets for reuse.

---

### Azure Synapse Analytics

- MONITOR WITH **Synapse Studio**, **Query Insights**, and **DMVs**.
- Profile slow queries using execution plans.
- Cache result sets to reduce repeated compute.

**Serverless SQL Tips:**

- Optimize file paths and avoid scanning full folders.
- Use schema-on-read with columnar formats like Parquet.
- Avoid SELECT * queries.

**Dedicated SQL Pool Tips:**

- Scale up only during peak hours.
- Pause pool during idle periods to reduce cost.
- Partition large fact tables for performance and cost.

---

**Azure Databricks**

- ENABLE **Cluster Logs** and monitor via Spark UI.
- Use **Job Clusters** for batch pipelines instead of always-on clusters.
- Set **auto-termination timeouts** on idle clusters.
- Enable **Photon runtime** for accelerated performance.

**Cost Controls:**

- Use spot instances for non-critical workloads.
- Monitor via Azure Monitor and Databricks REST APIs.
- Profile jobs to minimize shuffle and serialization overhead.

---

**Azure Data Lake Storage**

- TRACK BLOB COUNT and average size.
- Monitor read/write throughput.
- Transition cold data to **Cool** or **Archive** tiers with lifecycle policies.

**Lifecycle Policy Example (JSON):**

```
{
"rules": [
{
"enabled": true,
"name": "archive-inactive-logs",
"definition": {
"filters": {
"prefixMatch": ["logs/"]
},
"actions": {
"baseBlob": {
"tierToCool": { "daysAfterModificationGreaterThan": 30 },
"tierToArchive": { "daysAfterModificationGreaterThan": 180 }
}
}
}
}
]
}
```

## Alerts and Automation

AZURE MONITOR SUPPORTS automated actions triggered by performance or cost thresholds.

**Alert Types:**

- CPU USAGE EXCEEDS 80% on Synapse Pool
- ADF pipeline run takes > 30 minutes
- Daily cost exceeds forecast by 20%
- ADLS egress crosses defined budget

**Automated Actions:**

- Send email or SMS to administrators
- Trigger Azure Logic App to scale resource
- Auto-pause Databricks or Synapse compute
- Run PowerShell script to archive data

**Example Alert Rule (CLI):**

```
az monitor metrics alert create \
—name "HighADFDuration" \
—resource myDataFactory \
—condition "avg ActivityRunDuration > 1800" \
—window-size 15m \
—evaluation-frequency 5m \
```

—action emailAdminGroup

---

## Organizational Cost Governance

1. **Set Departmental Budgets**

    ○ Define cost limits per subscription, resource group, or tag.

    ○ Delegate reporting responsibilities to budget owners.

2. **Enable Cost Anomaly Alerts**

    ○ Use Azure Advisor or Cost Management to detect unusual spikes.

3. **Centralized Chargeback**

    ○ Apply resource tags consistently.

    ○ Export cost data to CSV or Power BI for internal chargeback.

4. **Integrate with FinOps Tools**

    ○ Use Azure Cost Export APIs with third-party cost management tools.

---

## Best Practices Checklist

- ◈ IMPLEMENT RESOURCE tagging across all services.
- ◈ Enable diagnostic logs and route to Log Analytics.
- ◈ Set auto-termination on compute clusters.

- ◈ Use dashboards to visualize performance and spend trends.
- ◈ Leverage partitioning and pruning to reduce query costs.
- ◈ Establish lifecycle policies for cold data.
- ◈ Monitor for failed or long-running pipelines.
- ◈ Allocate budgets and configure alerts at team/project level.
- ◈ Analyze ADF, Databricks, and Synapse logs for idle usage patterns.

---

## Summary

MONITORING AND MANAGING performance and cost in Azure data environments is not a one-time task—it's an ongoing discipline that must be embedded into architecture, governance, and operational workflows. With Azure Monitor, Log Analytics, and Cost Management tools, data teams can gain visibility, ensure accountability, and take proactive steps to optimize both efficiency and spend. By establishing a culture of observability, organizations can maximize the return on their cloud data investments while maintaining speed, reliability, and compliance.

In the next chapter, we will explore governance and security, focusing on access control, encryption, auditability, and compliance frameworks that safeguard data and ensure organizational trust in a multi-tenant, cloud-native ecosystem.

# Chapter 5: Data Governance and Security

## Azure Role-Based Access Control (RBAC)

IN ANY CLOUD-SCALE data platform, data governance is inseparable from access control. With vast volumes of sensitive, regulated, and business-critical data residing in cloud-native services like Azure Data Lake Storage, Synapse Analytics, and Azure Data Factory, organizations must enforce robust, scalable, and auditable access management frameworks. Azure Role-Based Access Control (RBAC) is the primary mechanism within Azure for managing **who can access what** at various levels of granularity.

RBAC is a foundational governance tool, offering centralized identity-based control over Azure resources. This section delves into how RBAC works, its integration across the Azure data platform, best practices for implementation, and its role in securing data lakes, analytics services, and orchestration workflows.

---

### Understanding RBAC in Azure

AZURE RBAC IS A SYSTEM that provides **fine-grained access management** to Azure resources based on the roles assigned to users, groups, service principals, or managed identities.

**Key Concepts:**

- **Principal**: The identity requesting access (user, group, service principal, or managed identity).
- **Role Definition**: A set of permissions (e.g., read, write, delete) assigned to a role.

- **Scope**: The resource boundary within which the role applies (subscription, resource group, or individual resource).
- **Assignment**: A link between a principal, a role, and a scope.

RBAC operates at multiple hierarchical levels:

- **Management Group**: For enterprise-wide policies.
- **Subscription**: Governs all resources within a billing context.
- **Resource Group**: Common for data platform components grouped logically.
- **Resource**: Specific access to a single service like an ADLS container or Synapse workspace.

---

## Built-In Roles for Data Platforms

AZURE PROVIDES HUNDREDS of built-in roles, including those specific to data services. Some of the most relevant for data architecture include:

**General Roles:**

- **Owner**: Full access to all resources, including the ability to delegate.
- **Contributor**: Manage everything except access control.
- **Reader**: View-only access.

**Data-Specific Roles:**

- **Storage Blob Data Reader**: Read data from blob containers (e.g., ADLS Gen2).

- **Storage Blob Data Contributor**: Read, write, and delete blob data.
- **Synapse Administrator**: Full access to Synapse resources.
- **Synapse SQL Administrator**: Manage SQL pools and data.
- **Data Factory Contributor**: Manage data factory resources.
- **Purview Data Curator**: Manage metadata and glossary terms.

Each role maps to one or more **Azure Resource Provider operations**, such as:

Microsoft.Storage/storageAccounts/blobServices/containers/read

Microsoft.Synapse/workspaces/sqlPools/read

Microsoft.DataFactory/factories/pipelines/write

---

## Granting Access with RBAC

ACCESS IS GRANTED BY **assigning a role to a principal at a specific scope.** This can be done via the Azure Portal, CLI, ARM templates, or Terraform.

**Example: Assign Reader Role via Azure CLI**

```
az role assignment create \

—assignee user@company.com \

—role "Reader" \

—scope /subscriptions/<sub-id>/resourceGroups/my-rg
```

**Terraform Example:**

```
resource "azurerm_role_assignment" "storage_reader" {

scope = azurerm_storage_account.datalake.id

role_definition_name = "Storage Blob Data Reader"

principal_id = azuread_user.analyst.id

}
```

## Managed Identities and RBAC

**MANAGED IDENTITIES** are a secure way for Azure resources to authenticate without managing secrets or credentials. When combined with RBAC, they enable seamless and secure interactions between services.

Use cases include:

- ADF pipelines reading from ADLS.
- Databricks accessing Synapse.
- Synapse querying ADLS data.

**Enabling a Managed Identity (ADF Example):**

1. Enable system-assigned identity in ADF.
2. Grant "Storage Blob Data Contributor" on the ADLS container.
3. ADF can now copy data without hardcoded credentials.

## RBAC for Azure Data Lake Storage Gen2

ADLS GEN2 INTRODUCES **POSIX-style ACLs** alongside RBAC. While RBAC controls access at the **resource level**, ACLs control access **within the file system hierarchy**.

**Best Practice**: Use RBAC for broader access scopes and ACLs for fine-grained access within the container.

**Typical Pattern:**

- RBAC at the container level (e.g., contributor role).
- ACLs on directories for team-based control (e.g., /raw/hr/ accessible only to HR team).

**Managing ACLs with Azure CLI:**

```
az storage fs access set \

—acl "user::rwx,group::r—,other::—-" \

—path "raw/hr/" \

—account-name mystorageaccount \

—file-system raw
```

RBAC controls **access to the container itself**, while ACLs control **access to directories and files** inside the container.

---

## RBAC in Synapse and SQL

SYNAPSE SUPPORTS BOTH **Azure RBAC** and **SQL-based access control**.

**Azure RBAC**:

• Controls access to the workspace, pipelines, Spark pools, etc.

**SQL Authorization**:

• Used within Dedicated SQL Pools.

• Roles like db_datareader, db_owner, or custom roles.

• Row-level security (RLS) and column-level security (CLS) supported.

**Use Case**:

• Analysts may have read-only access to a workspace via RBAC.

• Developers have write access to SQL tables via T-SQL GRANT statements.

---

## RBAC in Azure Data Factory

RBAC ROLES CONTROL:

• Creation and execution of pipelines.

• Management of triggers and linked services.

**Key Roles**:

• Data Factory Contributor: Full pipeline control.

• Data Factory Reader: Monitor but not modify pipelines.

**Managed Identity Flow Example**:

• Assign "Contributor" to ADF on the Synapse workspace.

• ADF pipeline runs stored procedures on Synapse using identity-based authentication.

---

## Security Best Practices

1. **Least Privilege Principle**
   Assign only the minimum required roles for each user or service.
2. **Use Groups and Azure AD**
   Assign roles to Azure AD groups instead of individual users.
3. **Audit Role Assignments**
   Use Azure Activity Logs to track RBAC changes.
4. **Review Access Regularly**
   Implement access review policies for privileged roles.
5. **Tag Sensitive Resources**
   Use tagging to group and monitor high-risk data sources.
6. **Integrate with Azure Policy**
   Prevent over-permissive roles using policy enforcement (e.g., deny "Owner" at subscription scope).

---

## Monitoring and Auditing RBAC

USE **Azure Activity Logs** to track:

- Role assignments and deletions.
- Privilege escalation attempts.
- Unauthorized access attempts.

**KQL Example – List all recent role changes:**

AuditLogs

| where ActivityDisplayName contains "Role"

| summarize count() by ActivityDisplayName, TargetResources

**Azure Policy Example:**

```
{
"if": {
"field": "roleDefinitionId",
"equals": "/providers/Microsoft.Authorization/roleDefinitions/<owner-role-id>"
},
"then": {
"effect": "deny"
}
}
```

## RBAC and Compliance

RBAC HELPS FULFILL compliance requirements like:

- **HIPAA**: Limit access to protected health information.
- **GDPR**: Enforce data minimization and access transparency.
- **ISO 27001**: Define and control access roles and privileges.

**Azure Blueprint Integration:**

- Use blueprints to automate deployment of RBAC-compliant environments.
- Ensure consistent access policies across environments.

## Summary

AZURE ROLE-BASED ACCESS Control is a critical pillar of a secure, governable, and scalable data architecture. By leveraging RBAC in conjunction with managed identities, directory-based roles, and file-level ACLs, organizations can enforce consistent and auditable access policies across their entire Azure data estate. Whether you're protecting raw ingestion zones, securing sensitive SQL views, or controlling pipeline execution, RBAC ensures only the right users and services have access—at the right scope and time.

The next section will explore encryption and key management strategies in Azure to further fortify your data lake and analytics platform, covering at-rest and in-transit encryption, customer-managed keys, and best practices for using Azure Key Vault.

# Data Encryption and Key Management

IN CLOUD-NATIVE DATA architectures, safeguarding sensitive information is both a legal necessity and a strategic imperative. As enterprises migrate workloads to platforms like Azure Data Lake Storage, Synapse Analytics, Azure SQL, and Azure Blob Storage, the need for robust encryption strategies has never been more critical. Encryption protects data from unauthorized access and ensures compliance with a wide array of regulations, including GDPR, HIPAA, ISO 27001, and CCPA. Equally important is **key management**, which governs how encryption keys are generated, stored, rotated, and revoked.

Azure provides a comprehensive framework for both **encryption at rest** and **encryption in transit**, using services such as **Azure Storage Encryption**, **Azure Disk Encryption**, **Azure SQL Transparent Data Encryption (TDE)**, and **Azure Key Vault** for centralized key management. This section explores the principles of encryption in Azure, types of encryption mechanisms, managed and customer-managed key strategies, auditability, integration with services, and best practices for securing your data at every stage of its lifecycle.

## Fundamentals of Encryption

**ENCRYPTION** is the process of converting data into a coded form to prevent unauthorized access. It is applied at multiple levels:

1. **At Rest**: Protects data stored on disk (e.g., in ADLS, SQL, Synapse).
2. **In Transit**: Protects data as it moves across networks (e.g., API calls, replication).
3. **In Use**: Emerging capabilities such as confidential computing.

**Key Management** governs how the cryptographic keys used in encryption are controlled, including:

- Generation
- Rotation
- Revocation
- Access control
- Audit logging

## Encryption at Rest

AZURE ENCRYPTS ALL data at rest by default using **Azure Storage Encryption**. This is enabled across all storage services including:

- Azure Data Lake Storage Gen2
- Azure Blob Storage
- Azure SQL Database
- Azure Synapse Analytics
- Azure Cosmos DB

**Types of Encryption Keys:**

1. **Platform-Managed Keys (PMKs)**:
   Default encryption managed entirely by Microsoft. Suitable for general workloads.
2. **Customer-Managed Keys (CMKs)**:
   Hosted in **Azure Key Vault**, these offer full control over access, rotation, and auditing.
3. **Customer-Provided Keys (CPKs)**:
   Supplied with each API call for highly specialized scenarios (e.g., financial and government data compliance).

---

## Azure Key Vault Integration

AZURE KEY VAULT IS the primary tool for **storing and controlling access** to encryption keys, secrets, and certificates.

**Key Features:**

- Hardware Security Module (HSM)–backed protection
- Soft delete and purge protection
- Key rotation policies
- Integration with storage, SQL, ADF, and more

**Creating a CMK in Key Vault (Terraform):**

```
resource "azurerm_key_vault_key" "cmk" {
name = "data-encryption-key"
key_vault_id = azurerm_key_vault.main.id
key_type = "RSA"
key_size = 2048
expiration_date = "2026-12-31T23:59:59Z"
}
```

**Assigning a CMK to ADLS:**

```
resource "azurerm_storage_account_customer_managed_key" "example" {
storage_account_id = azurerm_storage_account.datalake.id
key_vault_key_id = azurerm_key_vault_key.cmk.id
}
```

---

## Encryption in Transit

ALL AZURE SERVICES support encryption for data in transit using **Transport Layer Security (TLS) 1.2** or higher. This includes:

- HTTPS communication between services
- Secure transfer between client apps and storage
- Encrypted ingestion from on-premises sources

**Service-specific controls:**

- **Azure Storage**: Enforce HTTPS-only connections.
- **Synapse**: Use encrypted endpoints for SQL and Spark.
- **SQL Database**: Enforce TLS connections using connection string settings.

**Azure CLI Example to Require Secure Transfer:**

```
az storage account update \
—name mystorageaccount \
—resource-group myRG \
—https-only true
```

---

## Encryption for Specific Azure Services

### Azure Data Lake Storage Gen2

- ENABLED BY DEFAULT with PMK.
- CMK support requires Azure Key Vault + access policy assignment.
- Supports encryption of blob containers, directories, and files.
- ADLS also supports secure file deletion and audit logging via diagnostic settings.

**Azure Synapse Analytics**

- SQL POOLS AND SPARK compute support TDE.
- Synapse-managed TDE by default; CMK can be configured via Key Vault.
- Encrypted connections required for client access.
- Data movement via PolyBase or ADF maintains encryption during transit.

**Synapse TDE with CMK:**

```
ALTER DATABASE mydb

SET ENCRYPTION ON

WITH ROLLBACK IMMEDIATE;
```

**Azure SQL Database**

- TRANSPARENT DATA Encryption (TDE) enabled by default.
- Option to bring your own key (BYOK) via Key Vault.
- Column-level encryption and Always Encrypted supported for additional protection.

**Enable TDE with Customer Key (Portal):**

1. Import key into Key Vault.
2. Grant SQL Server access to the Key Vault.
3. Configure TDE in the SQL database blade.

---

## Key Rotation and Expiration

BEST PRACTICE DICTATES that encryption keys must be **rotated regularly** to reduce risk exposure.

Azure Key Vault supports:

- Manual key rotation
- Programmatic rotation using Azure Functions
- Upcoming support for auto-rotation policies

**Key Rotation Strategy:**

- Create a new version of the key in Key Vault.
- Update the associated service to use the new key version.
- Deactivate old key version after grace period.

---

## Audit Logging and Access Control

SECURITY AND COMPLIANCE require full **audit trails** for key usage:

- **Azure Monitor** and **Log Analytics** can collect Key Vault operation logs.
- Alerts can be configured for unauthorized access attempts or expired keys.
- RBAC controls define who can read, create, or delete keys and secrets.

**Example: KQL Query for Key Access**

AzureDiagnostics

| where ResourceType == "VAULT" and OperationName == "GetKey"

| summarize count() by CallerIpAddress, Identity, ResultType

## Encryption for Machine Learning and Analytics Workloads

- AZURE DATABRICKS supports encrypted Delta tables.
- Azure ML uses encrypted storage and secure compute (GPU/TPU).
- Secure scoring endpoints via HTTPS.
- Data lineage and intermediate datasets stored in encrypted containers.

**Model Encryption Strategy:**

- Encrypt training datasets at rest in ADLS.
- Encrypt model artifacts during registration and deployment.
- Use secure scoring with Key Vault–protected API keys.

## Compliance Considerations

ENCRYPTION AND KEY management are essential to complying with global data protection regulations:

| Compliance Standard | Encryption Requirement |
|---|---|
| GDPR | Pseudonymization, access control, audit logging |
| HIPAA | Encryption of PHI at rest and in transit |
| ISO 27001 | Key lifecycle policies, access control |
| CCPA | Data protection and anonymization |
| FedRAMP | FIPS 140-2 validated encryption |

Azure meets these requirements with built-in encryption, Key Vault controls, and detailed auditing.

---

## Best Practices for Encryption and Key Management

- ✧ USE **CMKs** in Azure Key Vault for regulated and sensitive data.
- ✧ Enforce **HTTPS-only** across all endpoints.
- ✧ Rotate keys regularly and enforce expiration dates.
- ✧ Enable **audit logging** and integrate with SIEM tools.
- ✧ Implement **network rules** and **private endpoints** for Key Vault access.
- ✧ Avoid embedding keys or secrets in code—use managed identity and Key Vault.
- ✧ Classify and encrypt data based on **sensitivity labels.**

---

## Summary

DATA ENCRYPTION AND key management are non-negotiable foundations of a secure, enterprise-grade data platform. Azure provides robust, flexible mechanisms to ensure that data is protected both at rest and in transit, while Azure Key Vault offers fine-grained control and auditability for encryption keys. By leveraging these capabilities—combined with best practices in access control, auditing, and compliance alignment—organizations can ensure the confidentiality, integrity, and availability of their data assets in the cloud.

In the next section, we will explore how to implement full data lineage and auditing in Azure, enabling traceability, governance, and transparency across every stage of the data lifecycle.

## Implementing Data Lineage and Auditing

AS ORGANIZATIONS ACCELERATE their adoption of cloud-based data platforms, the need for visibility into the movement, transformation, and usage of data becomes paramount. Data lineage and auditing are critical capabilities for achieving enterprise-level data governance, operational transparency, and regulatory compliance. In Azure, these capabilities are supported through a combination of integrated tools—including Azure Purview (now part of Microsoft Purview), Azure Monitor, Azure Data Factory, Synapse Analytics, and Azure Activity Logs—working together to create a comprehensive observability and traceability framework.

This section explores how to implement and operationalize end-to-end data lineage and auditing within Azure. It covers the architecture of lineage capture, audit logging strategies, integration with pipeline orchestration tools, regulatory use cases, and best practices to ensure robust oversight and accountability in modern data ecosystems.

## What is Data Lineage?

**DATA LINEAGE** refers to the ability to trace the origin, movement, and transformation of data across systems. It answers key questions such as:

- Where did this data come from?
- What processes modified it?
- Who accessed or altered it?
- Where is it used downstream?

Lineage provides transparency for:

- Troubleshooting and debugging pipeline failures
- Understanding the impact of schema changes
- Ensuring data quality and trustworthiness
- Supporting compliance with regulations (e.g., GDPR, HIPAA)

---

## What is Auditing?

**AUDITING** refers to the logging and analysis of access and modification events within a data platform. It enables:

- Accountability through user and system activity tracking
- Detection of unauthorized access or suspicious behavior
- Proof of compliance for legal and regulatory standards

Together, lineage and auditing create a comprehensive **data observability layer**—vital for data stewards, engineers, analysts, and compliance officers.

---

## Data Lineage Architecture in Azure

AZURE SUPPORTS LINEAGE and auditing via a **decentralized model**, where multiple services emit telemetry data that can be aggregated, visualized, and analyzed centrally.

**Core Components:**

1. **Azure Purview (Microsoft Purview)**
    - Visual lineage graphs
    - Metadata and transformation tracking
    - Business glossary and asset linking
2. **Azure Data Factory**
    - Automatically emits pipeline lineage into Purview
    - Tracks sources, transformations, and outputs
3. **Azure Synapse Analytics**
    - Integration with Purview for external table lineage
    - Tracks SQL transformation history (via DMVs)
4. **Azure Monitor + Log Analytics**
    - Captures detailed activity logs and diagnostics
    - Supports KQL-based audit analysis
5. **Azure Activity Logs**

○ Captures role assignments, policy changes, and resource modifications

---

## Setting Up Lineage with Azure Purview

1. **Register Data Sources**

○ Register ADLS, Synapse, Azure SQL, Power BI, and more.

2. **Run Scans with Lineage Enabled**

○ Set up recurring scans on each source.

○ Enable lineage capture for pipeline, SQL, and transformation assets.

3. **Integrate ADF and Synapse Pipelines**

○ Use built-in Purview connectors in ADF and Synapse.

○ Purview auto-generates lineage from activities (e.g., copy, data flow, SQL).

4. **View Lineage Graphs**

○ Navigate to a dataset in Purview.

○ Visualize upstream and downstream dependencies.

**Example Use Case:**

- A data steward views the lineage of a curated customer_orders Parquet file.

- The graph shows ingestion from SQL Server, transformation in ADF, and output to Power BI.
- The steward can click on any step to view schema, modification history, and access patterns.

---

## Logging and Auditing with Azure Monitor

AZURE MONITOR ALLOWS centralized logging across services. Logs can be queried with **Kusto Query Language (KQL)** and exported to SIEM tools like Sentinel.

**Example: Log ADF Activity Execution**

```
ADFACTIVITYRUN
| where Status == "Failed"
| summarize failures = count() by PipelineName, ActivityName, ErrorCode
```

**Example: Audit ADLS File Access**

```
STORAGEBLOBLOGS
| where OperationName == "GetBlob" and StatusCode == 200
| project TimeGenerated, CallerIpAddress, Uri, Identity
```

**Enable Diagnostic Settings**

EACH AZURE RESOURCE (e.g., ADLS, Key Vault, Synapse) allows configuration of diagnostic settings to:

- Send logs to Log Analytics

- Archive to Storage Account
- Stream to Event Hub

**CLI Example:**

az monitor diagnostic-settings create \

—resource <resource-id> \

—workspace <log-analytics-workspace-id> \

—name "enable-logging"

---

## Implementing End-to-End Lineage in Pipelines

TO CAPTURE LINEAGE across ingestion, transformation, and serving layers:

1. **Ingestion (ADF/Databricks):**
   - Log source dataset IDs, source schemas, and timestamped metadata into a lineage table.
   - Use parameters in pipelines to tag data flows with IDs.
2. **Transformation (Synapse/Databricks):**
   - Maintain transformation audit logs with SQL INSERT INTO lineage_log statements.
   - Use notebook logging (e.g., mlflow, dbutils.notebook.exit) to register outputs.
3. **Serving (Power BI/Synapse Views):**
   - Tag semantic models with glossary terms from Purview.

  ○ Register dashboards as consumers in lineage graphs.

4. **Storage (ADLS):**

  ○ Use structured folder naming (e.g., year=2025/month=05/) to trace version lineage.

  ○ Embed metadata files (_SUCCESS, _schema.json) alongside data.

---

## Compliance Use Cases Enabled by Lineage and Auditing

| Requirement | Solution Components |
|---|---|
| **GDPR Right to Know** | Purview lineage shows where customer data flows |
| **HIPAA Access Audit** | Log Analytics shows who accessed PHI |
| **ISO 27001 Change Control** | Activity Logs show resource and policy changes |
| **CCPA Deletion Tracking** | Data deletion logged across storage and queries |

## Integrating Lineage with CI/CD and DevOps

- USE AZURE DEVOPS pipelines to **validate lineage** as part of code promotion.

- Integrate Purview scans post-deployment to auto-capture schema and lineage.

- Use test environments to simulate lineage before promoting to production.

**Example CI Step:**

```
- task: AzureCLI@2

inputs:

scriptType: bash

scriptLocation: inlineScript

inlineScript: |

az purview account scan-run create—scan-name full-scan—resource-name my-purview
```

## Best Practices for Lineage and Auditing

- ◈ **Automate scans** using scheduled jobs or deployment hooks.
- ◈ **Use data asset naming conventions** to unify lineage across systems.
- ◈ **Implement metadata propagation** through ADF/Databricks transforms.
- ◈ **Centralize logs** in Log Analytics for correlation across services.
- ◈ **Assign roles and responsibilities** for lineage validation.
- ◈ **Visualize lineage** to understand blast radius before making changes.
- ◈ **Use tags and annotations** for versioning and classification.

## Summary

IMPLEMENTING ROBUST data lineage and auditing is essential for maintaining trust, accountability, and operational clarity in cloud-scale data platforms. With tools like Azure Purview, Azure

Monitor, and Log Analytics, enterprises can build a detailed, dynamic, and visual view of how data moves through their systems. When lineage and audit data are tightly integrated into pipeline orchestration, governance workflows, and compliance strategies, organizations are better equipped to respond to regulatory mandates, manage change, and ensure that data remains a valuable and trusted asset.

In the next section, we will explore how to ensure data privacy, security, and compliance alignment with global regulations such as GDPR, HIPAA, and CCPA using Azure-native controls and governance tooling.

## Compliance with GDPR and Other Regulations

IN TODAY'S GLOBAL DIGITAL economy, compliance with data protection regulations is not just a legal obligation but also a competitive differentiator and an enabler of user trust. Enterprises that operate in regulated industries or handle sensitive personal data must adhere to evolving regional and sectoral regulations such as the **General Data Protection Regulation (GDPR)**, **Health Insurance Portability and Accountability Act (HIPAA)**, **California Consumer Privacy Act (CCPA)**, **Financial Industry Regulatory Authority (FINRA)**, and others. Azure offers a wide suite of built-in tools, configurations, and integrations to help organizations architect their data lakes and analytical environments to meet these requirements in a secure and auditable manner.

This section explores the practical application of compliance frameworks within an Azure-based data architecture. We'll walk through regulatory principles, controls mapped to Azure services, implementation techniques across storage, compute, and pipelines, and strategies for documentation, automation, and validation. Whether you are handling patient health data, financial transactions, or consumer behavioral analytics, this section equips you with the tools to ensure lawful, secure, and traceable data handling.

---

## Core Regulatory Concepts

DESPITE VARIATIONS in geographic scope and industry focus, most compliance regulations are centered around a few key data protection principles:

- **Data Minimization**: Collect only what is necessary.
- **Purpose Limitation**: Use data only for the stated purpose.
- **Storage Limitation**: Retain data only as long as required.
- **Integrity and Confidentiality**: Protect data against unauthorized access or breaches.
- **Accountability and Transparency**: Maintain documentation of compliance activities and make data handling transparent to users.
- **Data Subject Rights**: Provide users with rights such as access, rectification, erasure (right to be forgotten), and data portability.

Azure provides native tooling to enforce, monitor, and audit these principles across services.

---

## Implementing GDPR Principles on Azure

### 1. Lawfulness, Fairness, and Transparency

USE **Azure Purview** to:

- Document data classifications and privacy attributes.

- Attach business glossary terms indicating sensitivity or purpose.
- Map assets to departments and legal bases for processing.

**Example**: Label columns like email, national_id, or medical_record_number as PII or PHI.

Enable **Azure Policy** and **Azure Blueprints** to enforce and track compliance across resource deployments.

---

**2. Purpose Limitation and Data Classification**

ENSURE THAT INGESTION pipelines tag data by purpose at the time of entry into the data lake.

**Techniques**:

- Create container/folder paths in ADLS that reflect purpose:

/raw/customer_feedback/ vs. /raw/marketing_insights/

- Use metadata tagging in Purview to align datasets with business use cases.

**Azure Tagging Example**:

az resource tag—tags Purpose=Marketing Compliance=GDPR—name mydataset—resource-group myRG

---

**3. Data Minimization**

AVOID UNNECESSARY DATA ingestion or storage. Drop unused fields as early as possible.

**ADF Data Flow Example**:

- Use "Select" transformation to exclude non-essential columns.
- Filter PII fields before writing to intermediate zones.

**Best Practice**:

- Maintain separate environments for raw, pseudonymized, and anonymized data.
- Implement approval workflows for introducing new sensitive fields.

---

**4. Accuracy and Rectification**

SUPPORT USER-SUBMITTED data correction by:

- Implementing upsert and merge logic in data lakes.
- Enabling downstream syncing with updated values in Synapse or Power BI.

**Delta Lake Merge Example** (Databricks):

```
MERGE INTO customer_data AS target
USING corrections AS source
ON target.customer_id = source.customer_id
WHEN MATCHED THEN UPDATE SET *
WHEN NOT MATCHED THEN INSERT *
```

### 5. Storage Limitation and Data Retention

IMPLEMENT RETENTION policies and lifecycle management to automatically archive or delete data after its purpose expires.

**ADLS Lifecycle Policy Example:**

```
{
"rules": [
{
"enabled": true,
"name": "delete-old-data",
"definition": {
"filters": {
"prefixMatch": ["curated/"]
},
"actions": {
"baseBlob": {
"delete": {
"daysAfterModificationGreaterThan": 365
}
}
}
```

```
}
}
]
}
```

Use **Purview** or a metadata registry to associate each dataset with retention durations and legal requirements.

---

**6. Integrity and Confidentiality**

ENFORCE ENCRYPTION, access control, and audit logging across all data services.

**Controls to Enable**:

- Encryption at rest with CMKs via **Azure Key Vault**.
- Encryption in transit via **TLS 1.2** enforced on all endpoints.
- Role-Based Access Control (RBAC) and file-level ACLs in **ADLS Gen2**.
- Privileged access review using **Azure AD PIM**.
- Diagnostic settings to forward logs to **Log Analytics** or **SIEM** tools.

**Audit Access Example (KQL)**:

```
StorageBlobLogs
| where OperationName == "GetBlob" and Uri contains "curated/personal"
```

```
| summarize count() by Identity, TimeGenerated
```

**7. Accountability and Documentation**

MAINTAIN FULL AUDIT trails of processing activities:

- Use **Azure Activity Logs** for resource changes and role assignments.
- Use **ADF and Synapse pipeline logs** to track transformation activities.
- Store Data Protection Impact Assessments (DPIAs) in a centralized SharePoint or Azure Files repository.

Automate compliance documentation with:

- CI/CD pipelines that enforce tagging and policy validation.
- Scheduled scans in Purview that update lineage and classification.

## Supporting Other Regulations

### HIPAA (Health Insurance Portability and Accountability Act)

- ENCRYPT ALL PROTECTED Health Information (PHI) using CMKs.
- Use private endpoints for all services handling PHI.
- Enable access logging on all storage and processing services.
- Sign a Business Associate Agreement (BAA) with Microsoft.

**CCPA (California Consumer Privacy Act)**

- MAINTAIN CATALOGS of personal information.
- Enable access and deletion requests via API or app interface.
- Track and respond to opt-outs and usage requests.
- Use Azure API Management to secure and monitor external-facing data APIs.

**ISO 27001 / SOC 2 / FedRAMP**

- APPLY AZURE POLICIES and Blueprints aligned to control frameworks.
- Monitor compliance posture with **Microsoft Defender for Cloud.**
- Perform regular penetration testing and vulnerability scans.

## Tools for Compliance Automation

| Tool | Function |
|---|---|
| **Microsoft Purview** | Metadata, classification, and lineage management |
| **Azure Policy** | Enforce compliance across deployments |
| **Azure Blueprints** | Prepackaged policy sets and RBAC templates |
| **Azure Key Vault** | Manage and audit encryption keys |
| **Defender for Cloud** | Secure score and regulatory compliance assessments |
| **Azure Monitor & Logs** | Centralized auditing and alerting |
| **Azure AD** | Identity governance and access reviews |

## Sample Compliance Architecture for GDPR

1. **Ingestion**:
   - ADF pipeline with metadata tagging and minimal field selection
   - Logged activity with correlation ID per request
2. **Storage (ADLS Gen2)**:
   - Encrypted with CMK
   - Folder structured by purpose and retention policy
   - Audit enabled with logs forwarded to SIEM
3. **Metadata (Purview)**:
   - Automated scanning
   - Tagged assets with purpose, owner, classification
   - Lineage mapping to all downstream reports
4. **Access Control**:
   - RBAC and ACLs
   - Azure AD group roles
   - Periodic access reviews
5. **Data Subject Requests (DSRs)**:
   - API to retrieve or delete personal data

- ○ Delta Lake merge operations to anonymize or erase
- ○ Audited actions with ADF activity logging

---

## Best Practices Checklist

- ◈ IDENTIFY AND CLASSIFY personal or sensitive data using Purview.
- ◈ Enforce encryption at rest and in transit across all services.
- ◈ Structure data lakes with purpose-labeled folders or containers.
- ◈ Tag data assets with purpose, owner, and retention policies.
- ◈ Implement lifecycle rules for automatic data expiry.
- ◈ Enable detailed access logging and integrate with SIEM.
- ◈ Design APIs or interfaces for DSRs (access, delete, rectify).
- ◈ Run regular compliance assessments and policy audits.
- ◈ Maintain documentation for data flows and protection controls.
- ◈ Use version-controlled infrastructure to enforce consistency.

---

## Summary

ACHIEVING COMPLIANCE with regulations like GDPR, HIPAA, and CCPA is a multifaceted challenge that demands an architectural, procedural, and cultural commitment to data protection. Azure provides a robust toolkit for implementing privacy-by-design principles through encryption, access control, data lineage, tagging, auditing, and policy enforcement. When properly configured, these tools enable organizations to process data responsibly, demonstrate compliance transparently, and respond quickly to regulatory demands.

In the next chapter, we shift focus from governance and security to data workflow orchestration—exploring how to design and manage resilient, traceable, and automated pipelines across complex data ecosystems using Azure Data Factory, Azure Synapse, and event-driven architectures.

# Chapter 6: Orchestrating Data Workflows

## Scheduling and Dependency Management in ADF

ORCHESTRATION IS THE backbone of scalable, automated data platforms. Without a centralized approach to scheduling, dependency tracking, and execution management, data pipelines become brittle, opaque, and difficult to scale. Azure Data Factory (ADF) is the principal orchestration service in the Azure ecosystem, providing robust capabilities for scheduling data flows, managing dependencies between tasks, controlling execution order, and integrating with other services through triggers, events, and pipelines. In modern data lake architectures, orchestrating workflows correctly ensures timely ingestion, reliable transformations, and a seamless flow of data across ingestion, curation, and analytics stages.

This section explores how ADF enables effective scheduling and dependency management across batch and streaming workloads. We will cover pipeline architecture, trigger types, dynamic scheduling, conditional flows, dependency modeling, activity chaining, reusability patterns, and monitoring. Whether you are orchestrating nightly data refreshes or coordinating real-time enrichment flows, mastering these features is essential for operational excellence in Azure.

---

### Core Concepts of ADF Orchestration

ADF PIPELINES ARE COMPOSED of multiple **activities**, organized into **pipelines**, and executed based on **triggers** or

**external events**. Activities can run sequentially or in parallel, and conditional logic can determine execution paths based on success or failure states.

**Key Orchestration Components:**

- **Pipeline**: Container for workflow logic.
- **Activity**: A single unit of execution (e.g., Copy, Notebook, Data Flow).
- **Trigger**: Defines when and how a pipeline is executed.
- **Dependency**: Control flow between activities using success/failure conditions.
- **Parameters**: Dynamic inputs that allow reuse and flexible execution.

---

## Scheduling Pipelines with Triggers

ADF SUPPORTS MULTIPLE types of triggers to initiate pipeline execution.

### 1. Schedule Trigger

USED FOR TIME-BASED execution.

**Example Use Case**: Run pipeline every day at 2 a.m.

```
{
"type": "ScheduleTrigger",
"typeProperties": {
```

```
"recurrence": {
"frequency": "Day",
"interval": 1,
"startTime": "2025-05-01T02:00:00Z",
"timeZone": "UTC"
}
}
}
```

Attach to pipeline using the portal or az datafactory trigger CLI.

**2. Event-Based Trigger**

EXECUTES PIPELINES based on file arrival or other blob events.

**Example Use Case**: Ingest a file as soon as it is uploaded to ADLS.

```
{
"type": "BlobEventsTrigger",
"typeProperties": {
"blobPathBeginsWith": "/raw/sales/",
"events": ["Microsoft.Storage.BlobCreated"],
"scope":
"/subscriptions/<sub-id>/resourceGroups/<rg>/providers/
Microsoft.Storage/storageAccounts/<account>"
```

}

}

### 3. Manual Trigger

FOR ON-DEMAND PIPELINE executions, often initiated via:

- Azure Portal
- REST API
- PowerShell
- Azure CLI
- Logic App or Power Automate integration

### 4. Tumbling Window Trigger

USED FOR FIXED-INTERVAL execution with dependency on previous window completion.

**Example Use Case:** Process hourly logs where each run depends on the previous run completing successfully.

```
{
"type": "TumblingWindowTrigger",
"typeProperties": {
"frequency": "Hour",
"interval": 1,
"startTime": "2025-05-01T00:00:00Z",
```

```
"maxConcurrency": 1,
"pipeline": {
"parameters": {
"windowStart": "@trigger().outputs.windowStartTime",
"windowEnd": "@trigger().outputs.windowEndTime"
}
}
}
}
```

## Dependency Management Between Activities

ACTIVITIES WITHIN A pipeline can be chained using dependencies based on:

- **Success**
- **Failure**
- **Completion**
- **Custom expressions**

**Example: Sequential Execution**

```
"dependsOn": [
{
"activity": "ExtractData",
```

```
"dependencyConditions": ["Succeeded"]
}
]
```

**Parallel Execution**: Omit dependsOn to allow activities to run concurrently.

**Conditional Execution**:

Use the **If Condition** activity to branch execution paths based on parameters or outcomes.

```
"expression": {
"value": "@equals(pipeline().parameters.runType, 'full')",
"type": "Expression"
}
```

## Dynamic Pipeline Parameterization

USE **parameters** and **variables** to make pipelines dynamic and reusable.

**Example Parameterized Copy Activity**:

```
"parameters": {
"sourcePath": "raw/sales/@{formatDateTime(utcNow(), 'yyyy/MM/dd')}/",
"targetPath": "curated/sales/"
}
```

Pass values at runtime from triggers or other activities.

Use **Set Variable**, **Append Variable**, and **Lookup** activities to manage pipeline state.

---

## Reusability and Modular Pipelines

FOR COMPLEX WORKFLOWS, use modularization patterns:

- Break large pipelines into smaller units.
- Use the **Execute Pipeline** activity to call sub-pipelines.
- Apply shared parameter templates to enforce consistency.

**Use Case**: A reusable pipeline for writing to ADLS from multiple sources.

**Main Pipeline:**

- Lookup metadata table
- ForEach activity looping over sources
- Call reusable pipeline with parameters

**Child Pipeline:**

- Copy data
- Apply dynamic partitioning
- Log success/failure

---

## Retry, Timeout, and Error Handling

RESILIENCE IS ESSENTIAL. Use built-in features for robustness:

- **Retry Policy**: Automatic retries on transient failures.

```
"policy": {
"retry": 3,
"timeout": "00:30:00",
"retryIntervalInSeconds": 120
}
```

- **Timeout**: Abort long-running or stuck operations.
- **On Failure Flow**: Trigger cleanup, alerting, or compensation logic.

**Use Case**: Send email on failure.

- Add Web Activity with Logic App endpoint under onFailure condition.

---

## Monitoring and Debugging Orchestrated Pipelines

ADF INCLUDES ROBUST monitoring tools:

- **Monitor tab**: View pipeline runs, durations, and outcomes.
- **Run Details**: Inspect input/output, logs, and activity duration.
- **Alerts**: Integrate with Azure Monitor for SLA enforcement and alerts.
- **Log Analytics**: Centralized logs and KQL queries for advanced analysis.

**Sample KQL Query**:

```
ADFActivityRun
| where Status != "Succeeded"
| summarize errorCount = count() by ActivityName, PipelineName
```

## Advanced Orchestration Scenarios

### 1. Pipeline Retry Loop

USE UNTIL ACTIVITY to retry a sub-pipeline until success or max attempts.

### 2. File-Driven Execution

USE LOOKUP + GET METADATA + ForEach for file-level parallel processing.

### 3. Metadata-Driven Framework

- STORE PIPELINE CONFIG in SQL table or Azure Table Storage.
- Lookup parameters for ingestion dynamically.
- Enables full pipeline abstraction.

### 4. DataOps Integration

- USE DEVOPS PIPELINES to deploy ADF resources via ARM templates or Bicep.
- Validate pipeline logic in dev before moving to prod.

- Implement rollback for failed deployments.

## Best Practices Checklist

- ◈ USE SCHEDULE AND event-based triggers for automation.
- ◈ Parameterize pipelines to enable reusability.
- ◈ Model dependencies explicitly for maintainability.
- ◈ Leverage sub-pipelines and modular orchestration.
- ◈ Implement retries and timeouts for resilience.
- ◈ Log and monitor all activities centrally.
- ◈ Use version control and CI/CD for pipeline lifecycle.
- ◈ Tag pipelines with metadata for traceability.
- ◈ Automate metadata-driven orchestration where feasible.
- ◈ Use alerting to detect anomalies and SLA violations.

## Summary

AZURE DATA FACTORY provides a powerful orchestration engine for automating data movement and transformation at scale. With rich support for scheduling, dependency management, modular design, dynamic parameters, and monitoring, ADF pipelines can be tailored to suit everything from simple ETL jobs to complex enterprise workflows. By applying best practices in orchestration design, organizations can ensure their data workflows are reliable, traceable, and maintainable—laying the foundation for consistent and compliant data operations.

In the next section, we will explore how to implement CI/CD for data pipelines using Azure DevOps, covering everything from environment promotion to release validation and deployment automation.

## CI/CD for Data Pipelines Using Azure DevOps

AS DATA PLATFORMS MATURE and scale, the complexity of data pipelines increases, making it critical to establish consistent, reliable, and automated deployment practices. Manual deployment of data pipelines is error-prone and unscalable, particularly when managing multiple environments like development, staging, and production. Continuous Integration and Continuous Delivery (CI/CD) practices—long adopted in software engineering—are equally essential in data engineering to ensure repeatability, traceability, and governance across the data lifecycle.

Azure DevOps provides a robust toolchain for implementing CI/CD pipelines tailored to Azure Data Factory (ADF), Synapse Pipelines, and other Azure services. With Git integration, build and release pipelines, infrastructure as code (IaC), and artifact management, Azure DevOps enables data teams to embrace DevOps principles like version control, automation, and testability in their ETL/ELT workflows.

This section covers the architecture, tooling, step-by-step implementation, environment management, parameterization strategies, promotion flows, and best practices for building CI/CD pipelines for Azure-based data workflows using Azure DevOps.

## Benefits of CI/CD in Data Engineering

• **Repeatability**: Deploy the same pipeline artifacts consistently across all environments.

• **Versioning**: Track changes to pipeline logic and rollback if necessary.

• **Separation of concerns**: Developers can focus on logic; DevOps handles deployment.

• **Auditability**: Maintain logs of who deployed what, when, and where.

• **Collaboration**: Enable distributed teams to contribute and review changes.

• **Agility**: Reduce time from development to production deployment.

---

## Git Integration with Azure Data Factory

ADF OFFERS NATIVE INTEGRATION with Git repositories hosted in Azure DevOps or GitHub.

**Steps to Integrate Git with ADF:**

1. Open ADF Studio.
2. Go to **Manage > Git Configuration**.
3. Select **Azure DevOps Git**.
4. Choose repo, collaboration branch (e.g., main), and publish branch (e.g., adf_publish).
5. Save configuration.

ALL PIPELINE JSONS, datasets, linked services, and triggers are now versioned in your Git repository.

**Folder Structure:**

/pipelines/

pipeline_copy_sales.json

/datasets/

/linkedServices/

/triggers/

arm-template-parameters-definition.json

## CI/CD Architecture

CI/CD FOR DATA PIPELINES typically consists of two stages:

1. **Continuous Integration (CI)**
   - Triggered by changes to the main branch.
   - Lint, validate, and compile the ARM templates.
   - Optionally deploy to dev or test.
2. **Continuous Delivery (CD)**
   - Triggered manually or by successful CI.
   - Deploy to staging or production using approved artifacts.
   - Use environment-specific parameters for configuration.

## Implementing CI/CD for ADF

### Step 1: Export ARM Template from ADF Studio

NAVIGATE TO **Manage** > **ARM Template** > **Export ARM Template**.

This generates:

- ARMTemplateForFactory.json
- ARMTemplateParametersForFactory.json

Include these in your Git repository for CI/CD deployments.

### Step 2: Create Azure DevOps CI Pipeline

CREATE A AZURE-PIPELINES.yml file:

```
trigger:
branches:
include:
- main
pool:
vmImage: 'ubuntu-latest'
variables:
- name: resourceGroup
value: 'rg-data-platform'
```

```
- name: dataFactoryName
value: 'adf-dev'
steps:
- task: AzureResourceManagerTemplateDeployment@3
inputs:
deploymentScope: 'Resource Group'
azureResourceManagerConnection: 'my-azure-service-connection'
subscriptionId: 'xxxxxxxx-xxxx-xxxx-xxxx-xxxxxxxxxxxx'
action: 'Create Or Update Resource Group'
resourceGroupName: '$(resourceGroup)'
location: 'East US'
templateLocation: 'Linked artifact'
csmFile: 'ARMTemplateForFactory.json'
csmParametersFile: 'ARMTemplateParametersForFactory.json'
overrideParameters: '-factoryName $(dataFactoryName)'
deploymentMode: 'Incremental'
```

## Environment Parameterization

USE ARM PARAMETERS to customize deployments per environment.

**Common Parameters to Override:**

- factoryName
- storageAccountName
- keyVaultUri
- environment (e.g., dev, staging, prod)

## Event-Driven Data Processing Patterns

EVENT-DRIVEN ARCHITECTURE (EDA) is a foundational design approach for modern, reactive, and scalable data platforms. Unlike traditional batch processing where data movement and transformation occur on fixed schedules, event-driven pipelines respond to changes in real time—ingesting, transforming, and acting on data as it arrives. In Azure, event-driven processing is supported through a rich ecosystem of services, including **Azure Event Grid**, **Azure Event Hubs**, **Azure Service Bus**, **Azure Functions**, **Azure Stream Analytics**, and **Azure Data Factory**.

This section explores event-driven patterns for building responsive data systems, including architectural models, common triggers, integration techniques, automation strategies, error handling, and governance considerations. We will walk through practical use cases and code examples that illustrate how to implement event-based orchestration in Azure Data Lake and analytics pipelines using cloud-native tools.

---

### Why Event-Driven Processing?

EVENT-DRIVEN ARCHITECTURES offer several advantages over batch systems:

- **Low latency**: React to changes immediately rather than waiting for batch windows.

- **Scalability**: Handle high-throughput data with elastic compute services.
- **Modularity**: Decouple producers and consumers through message brokers.
- **Extensibility**: Enable parallel processing across services and systems.
- **Cost efficiency**: Avoid unnecessary polling or scheduled job execution.

---

## Event Sources and Types

EVENTS CAN ORIGINATE from a wide variety of sources in the Azure ecosystem:

| Source | Event Type |
| --- | --- |
| Azure Blob Storage / ADLS | BlobCreated, BlobDeleted |
| Azure IoT Hub | Telemetry Events |
| Azure Event Hubs | Application telemetry, device data |
| Azure SQL Database | CDC, change tracking |
| Azure Cosmos DB | Change feed |
| Application APIs | Custom events (via Event Grid) |
| Power Platform / Logic Apps | Workflow events |

Events may be discrete (e.g., file upload) or streaming (e.g., clickstream, telemetry), and often require different handling mechanisms depending on scale, latency, and consistency needs.

---

## Event Ingestion with Azure Event Grid

**AZURE EVENT GRID** is a fully managed event routing service that enables reactive programming in Azure.

**Key Concepts:**

- **Event Sources**: Services that emit events (e.g., Storage, Key Vault).
- **Event Handlers**: Services that consume and process events (e.g., Azure Function, Logic App).
- **Topics and Subscriptions**: Topics receive events; subscriptions define routing logic.

**Example: Trigger ADF Pipeline on Blob Upload**

1. Blob uploaded to /raw/sales/2025/05/01/.
2. Event Grid receives Microsoft.Storage.BlobCreated event.
3. Event Grid subscription triggers a Logic App or Azure Function.
4. The function calls ADF REST API to run a pipeline.

**Event Subscription via CLI:**

```
az eventgrid event-subscription create \
—name sales-ingest-subscription \
—source-resource-id
"/subscriptions/<sub>/resourceGroups/<rg>/providers/
Microsoft.Storage/storageAccounts/<account>" \
—included-event-types Microsoft.Storage.BlobCreated \
—endpoint-type webhook \
—endpoint https://<function-url>
```

## Using Azure Data Factory with Event Triggers

AZURE DATA FACTORY supports **Event-based Triggers** natively for blob creation events.

**ADF Event Trigger JSON:**

```
{
"type": "BlobEventsTrigger",
"typeProperties": {
"blobPathBeginsWith": "raw/sales/",
"scope":
"/subscriptions/<sub-id>/resourceGroups/<rg>/providers/
Microsoft.Storage/storageAccounts/<storage>"
},
"pipelines": [
{
"pipelineReference": {
"referenceName": "IngestSalesBlob",
"type": "PipelineReference"
}
}
]
}
```

**Best Practices:**

- Filter on specific prefixes and suffixes.
- Validate blob name inside pipeline using Get Metadata.
- Use parameters to pass blob path dynamically.

## Real-Time Processing with Azure Stream Analytics

FOR HIGH-VOLUME, LOW-latency event streams, use **Azure Stream Analytics (ASA)**:

**Example Use Case**: Monitor IoT sensor data in real-time and trigger alerts for anomalies.

1. Stream events via Event Hub or IoT Hub.
2. ASA reads events, applies windowed aggregations.
3. ASA routes output to Power BI, ADLS, or Azure Function.

**ASA SQL Example:**

SELECT deviceId, AVG(temperature) AS avgTemp

INTO curated.device_temp

FROM iot_stream TIMESTAMP BY eventTime

GROUP BY deviceId, TumblingWindow(minute, 5)

**Output options**:

- Blob storage
- Synapse Analytics
- Power BI

- Azure Functions

---

## Integrating Azure Functions

AZURE FUNCTIONS PROVIDE lightweight, serverless processing in event-driven architectures.

**Use Cases:**

- Validate and enrich metadata.
- Trigger ADF pipelines.
- Route events to different systems.
- Send alerts or webhooks.

**Blob Trigger Example (Python):**

```
import logging

import azure.functions as func

def main(myblob: func.InputStream):

logging.info(f"Processing file: {myblob.name}")

# Trigger ADF pipeline or write to queue
```

Functions can be triggered from:

- Blob Storage
- Event Grid
- Event Hub
- Service Bus

• HTTP APIs

## Event Routing Patterns

### 1. File Arrival → Trigger Ingestion Pipeline

• EVENT: BLOBCREATED

• Handler: ADF pipeline

• Use when data lands sporadically in a staging zone

### 2. Real-Time Event → Immediate Enrichment and Storage

• EVENT: IOT TELEMETRY

• Handler: Stream Analytics → ADLS

• Use for high-volume, low-latency scenarios

### 3. Queue-Based Orchestration

• EVENT: CUSTOM EVENT pushed to Service Bus or Event Hub

• Handler: Logic App or Azure Function with durable messaging

• Use when ordering or retry handling is important

### 4. Event Grid Fan-Out

• EVENT: SINGLE BLOB triggers multiple downstream actions (e.g., data ingest + Slack alert)

• Use multiple Event Grid subscriptions for each handler

## Error Handling and Idempotency

HANDLING ERRORS IS essential in event-driven systems:

- Use retries and dead-letter queues (DLQ) in Event Hub and Service Bus.
- Implement idempotent operations in ADF and Functions to avoid duplicate writes.
- Store processing status and audit logs for every event.
- Use checkpointing for streaming jobs (e.g., in ASA or Databricks).

**Databricks Structured Streaming with Checkpointing:**

```
df.writeStream \
.format("delta") \
.option("checkpointLocation", "/checkpoints/sensor") \
.start("/curated/sensors/")
```

---

## Monitoring and Observability

USE AZURE-NATIVE TOOLS to monitor event-driven architectures:

- **Azure Monitor**: Centralized metrics and logs
- **Log Analytics**: Query errors, latencies, throughput
- **Event Grid Metrics**: Monitor event delivery and failures
- **Function App Logs**: Trace executions and exceptions

- **Stream Analytics Job Metrics**: Track dropped events, lag, throughput

**KQL Sample: Monitor BlobCreated Events**

```
AzureDiagnostics
| where OperationName == "BlobCreated"
| summarize count() by bin(TimeGenerated, 1h), Resource
```

## Security and Governance

- USE **Managed Identity** for secure function and pipeline triggers.
- Restrict Event Grid subscription endpoints with IP filtering or VNET integration.
- Enable **Private Endpoints** for storage and event processing.
- Use **Azure Policy** to enforce event-handling standards.

## Best Practices

- ◈ USE PREFIXES/SUFFIXES to filter blob events efficiently.
- ◈ Avoid duplicate processing—design for idempotency.
- ◈ Decouple producers and consumers with Event Grid or Service Bus.
- ◈ Monitor delivery failures and handle retries with DLQs.
- ◈ Document event contracts and payload schemas.
- ◈ Use tagging and metadata to track event sources and purposes.
- ◈ Integrate events with ADF for low-code orchestration.

- ◈ Use streaming analytics for real-time aggregation and transformation.

---

## Summary

EVENT-DRIVEN DATA PROCESSING transforms static, schedule-based systems into responsive, intelligent data platforms capable of real-time insights and automation. Azure's ecosystem—featuring Event Grid, Event Hubs, Stream Analytics, Azure Functions, and Data Factory—provides all the building blocks for scalable event-based architectures. By understanding and implementing event-driven patterns, data teams can unlock powerful new capabilities in analytics, automation, monitoring, and system integration, delivering faster and more flexible data products.

In the next section, we'll explore strategies for managing pipeline failures, implementing robust error handling, and setting up alerting mechanisms to ensure resilience and maintain high levels of data reliability and trust.

# Error Handling and Alerting Mechanisms

IN A MODERN DATA PLATFORM, reliability is non-negotiable. From data ingestion and transformation to model deployment and reporting, every layer of the pipeline must be designed to handle failure gracefully. Error handling and alerting mechanisms are critical for achieving operational resilience, maintaining data quality, and meeting service-level agreements (SLAs). Without robust mechanisms to catch, respond to, and recover from errors, data workflows can silently fail, leading to stale dashboards, missing insights, or compliance breaches.

This section details best practices and implementation patterns for detecting failures, implementing fallback logic, sending notifications, tracking retries, and integrating alerting into Azure-native data pipelines. Whether you're orchestrating ETL flows in Azure Data Factory, running real-time analytics with Azure Stream Analytics, or deploying machine learning models with Azure ML, this section provides a blueprint for ensuring your platform is self-monitoring, self-correcting, and transparent.

---

## Types of Errors in Data Pipelines

UNDERSTANDING ERROR types is the first step in designing effective handling strategies.

**1. Transient Errors**

- TEMPORARY FAILURES due to network issues or service throttling.
- Often resolved with retries.
- Examples: HTTP 429 (Too Many Requests), intermittent connection failures.

**2. Permanent Errors**

- FAILURES DUE TO misconfiguration, incorrect credentials, or schema mismatches.
- Require human intervention.
- Examples: Missing datasets, invalid query syntax.

**3. Logical Errors**

- ISSUES WITH DATA integrity or business rules.

- Detected by validation steps.
- Examples: Nulls in mandatory fields, negative values in financial fields.

**4. Systemic Failures**

- AFFECT ENTIRE SERVICES or regions.
- Require DR strategies or failover mechanisms.

---

## Error Handling in Azure Data Factory (ADF)

ADF PROVIDES BUILT-in control flow logic for error handling at the activity and pipeline level.

**Activity-Level Control Flow**

EACH ACTIVITY CAN DEFINE **dependencies** based on outcome:

```
"dependsOn": [
{
"activity": "IngestSalesData",
"dependencyConditions": ["Succeeded"]
},
{
"activity": "LogFailure",
"dependencyConditions": ["Failed"]
```

}

]

Use "dependencyConditions" to route execution based on:

- Succeeded
- Failed
- Skipped
- Completed

**Use Case: Retry and Notify on Failure**

"POLICY": {

"retry": 3,

"retryIntervalInSeconds": 60,

"timeout": "00:10:00"

}

If retries fail, route control to a **Web Activity** that posts to a Logic App or Teams webhook.

**Try-Catch with If Condition**

COMBINE **If Condition** and **Execute Pipeline** activities to implement try/catch-like logic.

1. Execute critical sub-pipeline.
2. Use **Set Variable** to track success/failure.
3. Use **If Condition** to decide whether to proceed or alert.

## Logging and Diagnostics

ENABLE **diagnostic settings** to export logs to:

- **Log Analytics Workspace**
- **Event Hub**
- **Storage Account**

Captured logs include:

- Pipeline runs
- Activity executions
- Trigger runs
- Integration runtime health

**Log Analytics Query Example**:

ADFActivityRun

| where Status == "Failed"

| project PipelineName, ActivityName, ErrorCode, ErrorMessage, RunId

Enable **run history retention** and configure alerts for repeated failures.

## Custom Error Logging

USE A **Stored Procedure** or **Append Data** activity to log errors into a central table.

**Error Logging Table Schema**

| Timestamp | PipelineName | Activity | ErrorCode | Message | Ru |
|---|---|---|---|---|---|
| UTC Date | String | String | String | NVARCHAR(MAX) | GU |

POPULATE USING EXPRESSIONS like:

"ErrorCode": "@{activity('IngestData').error.message}"

---

## Alerting Mechanisms

### 1. Azure Monitor Alerts

- SET ALERTS BASED on metric thresholds or log queries.
- Send notifications via email, SMS, webhooks, or ITSM tools.

**Metric Alert Example**:

- Condition: Pipeline Run Failures > 0 in the past 15 minutes.
- Action: Send to Email + Logic App.

**Log Alert Example (KQL)**:

```
ADFActivityRun

| where Status == "Failed"

| summarize count() by bin(TimeGenerated, 5m)
```

### 2. Integration with Logic Apps

USE A **Webhook** or **HTTP Request** action to automate alerting workflows.

**Alerting Workflow Example:**

- Trigger: HTTP request from ADF Web Activity.
- Actions:
    - Send email to operations team.
    - Create ticket in ServiceNow.
    - Post message to Microsoft Teams.

**3. Teams Notification via Webhook**

SEND ERROR MESSAGES to a Teams channel:

**Web Activity Payload Example:**

```
{
"text": "ADF Pipeline Failure: @{pipeline().PipelineName} - @{activity('IngestSalesData').error.message}"
}
```

## Handling Failures in Stream Analytics

- USE **diagnostic logs** for dropped events or serialization errors.
- Set up **job metrics alerts** for:
    - Late arrivals
    - Input drop rate
    - Output errors

**Stream Analytics Metrics to Watch**:

- Watermark Delay
- Deserialization Errors
- Runtime Errors

Use Azure Monitor to send alerts when thresholds are breached.

---

## Handling Errors in Azure Functions and Databricks

### Azure Functions

- IMPLEMENT TRY/CATCH logic in code.
- Log to Application Insights.
- Use **retry policies** with durable functions or queues.

### Databricks

- USE TRY/EXCEPT IN notebooks.
- Write failure logs to Delta or Log Analytics.
- Integrate with Azure Monitor via dbutils.notebook.exit() and exit codes.

---

## Reprocessing and Recovery

DESIGN PIPELINES TO support **idempotent** and **retriable** execution.

- Use checkpointing in Stream Analytics or Databricks.

- In ADF, pass window start/end times to re-run only affected slices.
- Store audit logs or watermark files in ADLS for incremental loads.

**Example Watermark Strategy:**

- Maintain a metadata table with last successful run time.
- Query delta from source systems based on that timestamp.
- Update watermark after success.

---

## Visual Monitoring and Dashboards

USE **Power BI**, **Azure Workbook**, or **Grafana** (via Log Analytics) to create operational dashboards.

Dashboard KPIs:

- Pipeline success rate
- Average execution time
- Failed activities by category
- Number of retries per pipeline
- Alerts triggered per week

---

## Best Practices Checklist

- ◈ USE ACTIVITY-LEVEL dependsOn logic to isolate and route failures.
- ◈ Log errors into centralized storage with metadata and timestamps.
- ◈ Alert on all failed runs using Azure Monitor and KQL.

- � Implement retry policies for transient errors.
- � Use idempotent processing logic to prevent duplication.
- � Monitor streaming jobs using runtime metrics.
- � Automate notifications using Logic Apps or Teams webhooks.
- � Maintain watermarks and audit tables for recovery.
- � Document failure scenarios and recovery playbooks.
- � Regularly test alerting and failure-handling workflows.

## Summary

BUILDING RELIABLE DATA workflows means anticipating failure and responding intelligently. By leveraging Azure's native monitoring, alerting, and logging capabilities—along with strategic design patterns like retry logic, idempotency, and metadata-driven auditing—data engineers can ensure resilience at scale. Proactive alerting keeps teams informed, while detailed logs and metrics provide the insight needed to resolve issues quickly and continuously improve data quality and delivery.

The next chapter explores how Azure integrates with machine learning and advanced analytics platforms, enabling end-to-end data science workflows within the cloud-native data lake architecture.

# Chapter 7: Machine Learning and Analytics Integration

## Enabling Data Science Workflows with Azure ML

INTEGRATING MACHINE learning into modern data platforms has become a standard requirement for organizations seeking to derive predictive insights, automate decisions, and personalize user experiences. Azure Machine Learning (Azure ML) provides a comprehensive suite of tools to support the end-to-end lifecycle of data science and machine learning workflows—from data preparation to model training, evaluation, and deployment. In the context of a data lake architecture, Azure ML plays a vital role in transforming curated data into actionable intelligence, enabling data scientists and engineers to collaborate within a unified, secure, and scalable ecosystem.

This section explores how to design, build, and manage data science workflows using Azure ML and how to integrate them effectively with Azure Data Lake Storage (ADLS), Azure Synapse Analytics, Azure Databricks, and orchestration tools like Azure Data Factory (ADF). We will cover key Azure ML concepts, workspace architecture, compute configuration, dataset registration, pipeline automation, MLOps practices, and security considerations.

---

### Azure ML Overview

AZURE ML IS A CLOUD-based platform for developing, training, deploying, and managing machine learning models at scale.

**Key Capabilities:**

- **Workspaces**: Logical containers for managing assets (models, experiments, datasets).
- **Experiments**: Track runs and parameters during model development.
- **Pipelines**: Automate and reproduce workflows.
- **Compute Targets**: Configure environments for training (CPU, GPU, AML Compute).
- **Model Registry**: Central store for versioned models.
- **Endpoints**: Serve models through REST APIs or batch inferencing.

---

## Architecting ML Workflows in Azure

**Typical Architecture:**

1. **Data Storage**: ADLS Gen2 stores raw, cleansed, and curated datasets.
2. **Data Access**: Registered datasets in Azure ML reference ADLS paths.
3. **Preprocessing**: Performed using Azure ML compute, Databricks, or Synapse.
4. **Training & Tuning**: Done on Azure ML compute clusters.
5. **Model Tracking**: Logs metrics and parameters via Experiments.
6. **Model Deployment**: To AKS (real-time) or Batch Endpoints (batch inference).
7. **Monitoring**: Tracked using Azure Application Insights and

custom logs.

---

## Setting Up Azure ML Workspace

CREATE AN AZURE ML workspace via CLI or ARM/Bicep:

```
az ml workspace create -g ml-rg -n ml-workspace—location eastus
```

Assign roles and permissions:

- Reader: For consumers of ML models.
- Contributor: For model developers.
- Owner: For admins managing compute and resources.

Enable diagnostic settings to log experiments and model deployments to Log Analytics.

---

## Working with Datasets

AZURE ML SUPPORTS TWO types of datasets:

- **Tabular**: Structured data for training (CSV, Parquet).
- **File**: For unstructured or image/text inputs.

**Registering a Dataset Example (Python SDK):**

```
from azureml.core import Workspace, Dataset

ws = Workspace.from_config()

datastore = ws.get_default_datastore()

dataset = Dataset.Tabular.from_delimited_files(path=(datastore, 'curated/sales.csv'))
```

```
dataset = dataset.register(workspace=ws,
name='sales_dataset',
create_new_version=True)
```

Use datasets in experiments, pipelines, or notebooks.

## Training Models in Azure ML

USE **Azure ML Experiments** to track hyperparameters, metrics, and outputs.

```
from azureml.core import Experiment, ScriptRunConfig, Environment
exp = Experiment(workspace=ws, name="sales-forecasting")
env = Environment.from_conda_specification(name="ml-env", file_path="conda.yml")
src = ScriptRunConfig(source_directory="training",
script="train.py",
compute_target="cpu-cluster",
environment=env)
run = exp.submit(config=src)
run.wait_for_completion(show_output=True)
```

**AutoML**

FOR BUSINESS ANALYSTS or teams seeking rapid prototyping, use **Azure AutoML** to automatically select algorithms and tune hyperparameters:

```
from azureml.train.automl import AutoMLConfig

automl_config = AutoMLConfig(task='regression',

primary_metric='r2_score',

training_data=dataset,

label_column_name='revenue',

iterations=10,

compute_target='cpu-cluster')

exp.submit(automl_config)
```

## Building and Running ML Pipelines

AZURE ML PIPELINES allow modular, repeatable workflows across stages:

1. Data preprocessing
2. Feature engineering
3. Model training
4. Model evaluation
5. Model registration

```
from azureml.pipeline.steps import PythonScriptStep

from azureml.pipeline.core import Pipeline
```

```
step1 = PythonScriptStep(name="prepare-data",
script_name="prepare.py",
arguments=["—input", dataset.as_named_input('input')],
compute_target="cpu-cluster",
source_directory="steps")
step2 = PythonScriptStep(name="train-model",
script_name="train.py",
compute_target="gpu-cluster",
source_directory="steps")
pipeline = Pipeline(workspace=ws, steps=[step1, step2])
pipeline.validate()
pipeline_run = pipeline.submit("model-training-pipeline")
```

## Model Registration and Deployment

AFTER TRAINING, MODELS are stored and versioned in the **Model Registry**.

```
model = run.register_model(model_name='sales_model', model_path='outputs/model.pkl')
```

**Deployment Options:**

- **Real-Time Inference**: Azure Kubernetes Service (AKS)
- **Batch Inference**: Azure Batch Endpoints or ADF pipeline

- **Edge Deployment**: Azure IoT Edge for edge scenarios

**Deploying to AKS:**

```
from azureml.core.webservice import AksWebservice, Webservice

aks_config = AksWebservice.deploy_configuration(cpu_cores=1, memory_gb=1)

service = Model.deploy(workspace=ws, name='sales-model-service', models=[model],

inference_config=inference_config,

deployment_config=aks_config,

deployment_target=aks_cluster)

service.wait_for_deployment(show_output=True)
```

## Integrating with Azure Data Factory and Synapse

USE **ADF** to:

- Trigger model training via Azure ML Pipelines
- Perform batch inference using Azure ML Endpoints
- Log predictions to ADLS or Synapse for BI reporting

**ADF Pipeline Activity Example:**

```
{

"name": "RunModelInference",

"type": "AzureMLExecutePipeline",

"dependsOn": [],
```

```
"typeProperties": {
"mlPipelineId": "sales-model-pipeline-id"
}
}
```

**Synapse Use Case:**

- Score customer churn within Spark pools using the registered model.
- Persist predictions in dedicated SQL pool for dashboarding.

## MLOps and CI/CD for ML

IMPLEMENTING MLOPS ensures continuous delivery of ML assets:

- **Model versioning and promotion**: Use Dev, Test, and Prod workspaces.
- **Code and data versioning**: Git + DVC + Azure Repos.
- **Test automation**: Validate model accuracy, latency, fairness.
- **CI/CD Pipelines:**
    - Trigger: Git commit or ADF signal
    - Build: Validate code, unit test
    - Deploy: Register model, deploy to endpoint, verify prediction

**Azure DevOps YAML Snippet:**

```
trigger:
branches:
include: ['main']
pool:
vmImage: 'ubuntu-latest'
steps:
- task: UsePythonVersion@0
inputs:
versionSpec: '3.8'
- script: |
pip install azureml-sdk
python scripts/register_model.py
```

## Security and Governance

- USE **Managed Identity** for secure access to ADLS and Key Vault.
- Store credentials and connection strings in **Azure Key Vault**.
- Enable **Private Link** and **network rules** for ML endpoints.
- Use **Purview** to track lineage of datasets and ML assets.
- Log prediction traffic via **Application Insights** for monitoring and diagnostics.

## Best Practices

- ⟐ USE MODULAR PIPELINE steps to improve reusability.
- ⟐ Leverage AutoML for rapid baseline benchmarking.
- ⟐ Store training metadata and metrics in Experiment logs.
- ⟐ Integrate ADF for scheduling and retraining workflows.
- ⟐ Version both data and code for reproducibility.
- ⟐ Automate deployments with CI/CD pipelines.
- ⟐ Monitor drift in input data and model predictions.
- ⟐ Secure data and model endpoints using RBAC and Key Vault.
- ⟐ Use Azure Monitor and Alerts to track service uptime and failures.
- ⟐ Log lineage of all inputs, transformations, and model outputs.

## Summary

AZURE MACHINE LEARNING enables powerful and scalable integration of data science into cloud-based analytics architectures. By leveraging its workspace structure, experiment tracking, pipeline orchestration, and deployment tools, data teams can collaborate efficiently, automate machine learning workflows, and deliver robust models into production with confidence. When combined with Azure Data Factory, Synapse Analytics, and DevOps tooling, Azure ML becomes a cornerstone of enterprise-grade, operationalized AI platforms—bridging the gap between raw data and intelligent applications.

In the next section, we will explore how to harness the power of Azure Databricks for advanced analytics, data engineering, and collaborative data science at scale.

## Leveraging Databricks for Advanced Analytics

DATABRICKS IS ONE OF the most powerful platforms for large-scale data engineering, data science, and machine learning in the cloud. Originally built on top of Apache Spark, Databricks simplifies the complexities of managing Spark clusters and adds collaborative notebooks, workflow orchestration, version control, machine learning lifecycle tools (MLflow), and seamless integrations with Azure services. For data architects and engineers building advanced analytics systems on Azure, Databricks plays a central role in unifying ETL pipelines, exploratory data science, and scalable model training.

This section explores how to integrate Databricks within an Azure-based data lake and analytics ecosystem. We will cover platform capabilities, architectural patterns, data ingestion and transformation, collaborative analytics, machine learning workflows, performance optimization, and security controls. The goal is to enable enterprise-grade use of Databricks as a backbone for advanced analytics.

---

### Databricks Architecture on Azure

AZURE DATABRICKS IS deployed as a first-party Azure service, offering:

- **Managed Spark Clusters**: Automated provisioning and scaling of clusters.

• **Notebooks Interface**: For Python, SQL, Scala, and R development.

• **Jobs and Workflows**: Schedule and orchestrate multi-step processes.

• **Delta Lake**: ACID-compliant lakehouse format for structured/ unstructured data.

• **MLflow**: Manage experiments, model versions, and deployments.

• **Unity Catalog**: Centralized governance for data and AI assets.

Databricks operates in your Azure Virtual Network (VNet), providing isolation, private link support, and enterprise-grade security.

---

## Connecting Databricks to Azure Data Lake Storage

TO ENABLE ACCESS TO data in ADLS Gen2, Databricks supports multiple authentication methods, most commonly:

• **Azure Service Principal** (SPN)

• **Managed Identity**

• **Access Keys (discouraged)**

• **Mounting via ABFS protocol**

**Mounting ADLS Gen2 (SPN Example):**

```
CONFIGS = {
"fs.azure.account.auth.type": "OAuth",
```

```
"fs.azure.account.oauth.provider.type":
"org.apache.hadoop.fs.azurebfs.oauth2.ClientCredsTokenProvider",

"fs.azure.account.oauth2.client.id": "<app-id>",

"fs.azure.account.oauth2.client.secret":
dbutils.secrets.get(scope="kv-scope", key="spn-secret"),

"fs.azure.account.oauth2.client.endpoint":
"https://login.microsoftonline.com/<tenant-id>/oauth2/token"

}

dbutils.fs.mount(

source =
"abfss://curated@<storage-account>.dfs.core.windows.net/",

mount_point = "/mnt/curated",

extra_configs = configs

)
```

Once mounted, you can access files using Spark APIs or directly with Databricks utilities:

```
df = spark.read.parquet("/mnt/curated/sales/2025/")
```

## Ingesting and Transforming Data

DATABRICKS SUPPORTS structured, semi-structured, and unstructured data ingestion at scale.

**Supported Formats:**

- CSV, JSON, PARQUET, ORC

- Avro, Delta Lake
- Images, audio, video (via UDFs)

**Batch Ingestion Example:**

```
RAW_DF = SPARK.READ.option("header", True).csv("/mnt/raw/sales/*.csv")

transformed_df = raw_df.withColumn("order_date", to_date(col("timestamp")))

transformed_df.write.format("delta").mode("overwrite").save("/mnt/curated/sales/")
```

**Streaming Ingestion Example:**

```
STREAM_DF = SPARK.READSTREAM.schema(schema).json("/mnt/raw/events/")

agg_df = stream_df \

.groupBy(window(col("timestamp"), "5 minutes")) \

.agg(avg("temperature").alias("avg_temp"))

agg_df.writeStream \

.format("delta") \

.option("checkpointLocation", "/mnt/checkpoints/temp") \

.start("/mnt/curated/temp_agg/")
```

## Delta Lake and the Lakehouse Pattern

**DELTA LAKE** brings ACID transactions, time travel, and scalable metadata to your data lake.

**Key Benefits:**

- TRANSACTIONAL GUARANTEES for concurrent writes.
- Support for UPDATE, DELETE, and MERGE statements.
- Schema enforcement and evolution.
- Native support for batch and streaming.

**Upsert (MERGE) Example:**

```
DELTA_TABLE = DELTATABLE.forPath(spark, "/mnt/curated/sales")

delta_table.alias("target").merge(

updates.alias("source"),

"target.id = source.id"

).whenMatchedUpdateAll().whenNotMatchedInsertAll().execute()
```

Use **time travel** for auditing and rollback:

```
df = spark.read.format("delta").option("timestampAsOf", "2025-05-01T00:00:00Z").load("/mnt/curated/sales")
```

## Collaborative Analytics with Notebooks

DATABRICKS NOTEBOOKS support real-time collaboration among data scientists, analysts, and engineers.

**Features:**

- MULTIPLE LANGUAGES in a single notebook (Python, SQL, Scala, R).
- Markdown support for documentation.
- Visualizations (bar, line, pie, scatter).
- Version control with Git integration.

**SQL Cell Example:**

```
SELECT customer_id, COUNT(*) AS orders
FROM delta.`/mnt/curated/sales`
GROUP BY customer_id
ORDER BY orders DESC
```

---

## ML Development and Experimentation

DATABRICKS INTEGRATES deeply with **MLflow** for tracking model development.

**Experiment Tracking:**

```
IMPORT MLFLOW
from sklearn.ensemble import RandomForestClassifier
```

with mlflow.start_run():

model = RandomForestClassifier()

model.fit(X_train, y_train)

mlflow.sklearn.log_model(model, "rf-model")

mlflow.log_metric("accuracy", accuracy_score(y_test, model.predict(X_test)))

**Model Registry:**

- STORE MULTIPLE VERSIONS.
- Transition between Staging and Production.
- Deploy as REST endpoints or batch jobs.

---

## Job Scheduling and Workflows

USE **Databricks Jobs** or **Workflows** for orchestrating pipelines:

- Define tasks (notebook, JAR, Python scripts).
- Configure dependencies between tasks.
- Set retries, notifications, and triggers.

**Workflow Example**:

- Task 1: Ingest raw data
- Task 2: Transform and write to Delta
- Task 3: Train model and log to MLflow
- Task 4: Notify via email

---

## Security and Governance

INTEGRATE WITH AZURE security features:

- **Azure Active Directory** for user authentication.
- **Unity Catalog** for fine-grained access control across databases and tables.
- **Credential passthrough** to use user's identity with ADLS.
- **Data masking and row-level security** with Unity Catalog policies.
- **Audit logs** routed to Log Analytics or Sentinel.

## Performance Optimization

**Tips:**

- USE **Auto Optimize** and **Optimize** commands on Delta tables.
- Partition large datasets by logical keys.
- Cache hot datasets using .cache().
- Use Photon Runtime for accelerated query performance.
- Monitor with **Ganglia**, **Spark UI**, and **SQL History**.

```
OPTIMIZE delta.`/mnt/curated/sales` ZORDER BY (order_date)
```

## Integration with Azure Ecosystem

| Azure Service | Integration Benefit |
|---|---|
| ADLS Gen2 | Scalable, secure data storage |
| ADF | Trigger Databricks notebooks via activities |
| Synapse | Share curated tables via shared metastore |
| Azure ML | Use as training compute or batch scorer |
| Purview | Register and trace data lineage |
| Monitor/LogAnalytics | Unified observability and alerting |

## Best Practices

- ◈ USE DELTA LAKE as the default table format.
- ◈ Mount ADLS using secure authentication (SPN or Managed Identity).
- ◈ Modularize code into reusable notebooks.
- ◈ Track experiments and metrics using MLflow.
- ◈ Partition and optimize large datasets.
- ◈ Schedule jobs using Workflows with retries.
- ◈ Use Unity Catalog for centralized governance.
- ◈ Enable audit logs for compliance.
- ◈ Monitor compute usage and optimize cluster lifecycles.
- ◈ Integrate with ADF or Azure ML for end-to-end automation.

## Summary

AZURE DATABRICKS EMPOWERS data teams with an interactive, scalable, and secure platform for advanced analytics and machine learning. It bridges the gap between big data engineering and collaborative data science through Delta Lake, MLflow, and integrated compute management. With support for structured streaming, powerful job orchestration, and tight integration with the Azure ecosystem, Databricks enables the realization of a modern lakehouse architecture—where raw data can be transformed into insights and predictive models in one unified platform.

In the next section, we explore how to build predictive data pipelines that combine engineering and science workflows, enabling seamless integration between training, scoring, and serving models at scale.

# Building Predictive Pipelines

PREDICTIVE PIPELINES are the convergence of traditional data engineering and modern machine learning, designed to operationalize insights by embedding predictive models into data workflows. These pipelines go beyond static reporting or historical analysis by incorporating dynamic models that forecast outcomes, classify behaviors, or recommend actions. On Azure, predictive pipelines integrate data lake storage, transformation layers, machine learning training and scoring components, and real-time or batch consumption endpoints—all orchestrated through services like Azure Data Factory (ADF), Azure ML, Databricks, and Azure Synapse.

This section outlines how to design, implement, and manage predictive data pipelines using the Azure ecosystem. Topics include data preparation, feature engineering, model training, batch/ real-time inference, model lifecycle management, versioning, CI/

CD integration, monitoring, and governance. By the end, you'll have a blueprint for delivering AI-enhanced data products in a scalable, maintainable, and auditable manner.

## What is a Predictive Pipeline?

A PREDICTIVE PIPELINE is a multi-stage automated process that:

- Ingests and transforms data.
- Applies feature engineering and enrichment.
- Trains and/or loads machine learning models.
- Generates predictions on new data.
- Stores predictions for use in dashboards, apps, or automated systems.

Predictive pipelines can run:

- **On schedule** (e.g. daily churn predictions).
- **On-demand** (e.g. ad-hoc forecasting).
- **Event-driven** (e.g. scoring new transactions in real time).

## Pipeline Architecture

TYPICAL ARCHITECTURE of a predictive pipeline:

1. **Data Ingestion**: ADLS, Azure SQL, APIs, or Event Hubs.
2. **Data Transformation**: Azure Databricks or ADF Data Flows.
3. **Feature Engineering**: SQL or Spark with versioned features.

4. **Model Loading**: From Azure ML Model Registry or MLflow.
5. **Prediction Generation**: Using Spark MLlib, scikit-learn, TensorFlow, or PyTorch.
6. **Prediction Storage**: Write to Delta, Synapse, Cosmos DB, or Power BI dataset.
7. **Monitoring and Logging**: Azure Monitor, Log Analytics, Application Insights.

---

## Example: Churn Prediction Pipeline

### Step 1: Data Preparation (Databricks or ADF)

```
DF = SPARK.READ.PARQUET("/mnt/curated/customers/")

df = df.withColumn("tenure", datediff(current_date(), col("signup_date")) / 30) \

.withColumn("is_active", col("last_login") >= date_sub(current_date(), 30))

df.write.mode("overwrite").format("delta").save("/mnt/features/churn/")
```

### Step 2: Feature Store Integration (Optional)

USE AZURE DATABRICKS Feature Store or custom metadata registry to manage feature consistency across training and scoring.

**Step 3: Model Training (Azure ML)**

FROM AZUREML.CORE IMPORT Experiment, ScriptRunConfig

config = ScriptRunConfig(source_directory="training",

script="train.py",

compute_target="cpu-cluster",

arguments=["—input_data", "/mnt/features/churn/"])

run = Experiment(workspace, "churn-training").submit(config)

**Step 4: Model Registration**

MODEL = RUN.REGISTER_model(model_name="churn_model", model_path="outputs/model.pkl")

---

## Batch Scoring in Predictive Pipelines

AFTER TRAINING, USE batch scoring to apply the model to new customer data.

**Option 1: Scoring with Azure ML Batch Endpoint**

FROM AZURE.AI.ML IMPORT MLClient

batch_inference_job = ml_client.batch_endpoints.invoke(

endpoint_name="churn-batch-endpoint",

input="/mnt/features/churn/",

```
output="/mnt/predictions/churn/"
)
```

**Option 2: Scoring in Databricks**

```
IMPORT MLFLOW.PYFUNC
model = mlflow.pyfunc.load_model("models:/churn_model/Production")
df = spark.read.parquet("/mnt/features/churn/")
predictions = model.predict(df.toPandas())
spark_df = spark.createDataFrame(predictions)
spark_df.write.format("delta").save("/mnt/predictions/churn/")
```

## Real-Time Inference

FOR LOW-LATENCY USE cases like fraud detection or product recommendation, deploy the model as a REST endpoint.

**Azure ML Real-Time Endpoint**

```
FROM AZUREML.CORE.WEBSERVICE import AciWebservice, Webservice
inference_config = InferenceConfig(entry_script="score.py", environment=env)
deployment_config = AciWebservice.deploy_configuration(cpu_cores=1, memory_gb=1)
```

```
service = Model.deploy(workspace, "churn-endpoint", [model], inference_config, deployment_config)

service.wait_for_deployment(show_output=True)
```

Call the endpoint via REST:

```
curl -X POST https://<endpoint>/score \

-H "Content-Type: application/json" \

-d '{"customer_id": "C123", "features": {...}}'
```

## Orchestrating Predictive Pipelines with ADF

USE ADF TO STITCH TOGETHER pipeline steps across environments and services.

**Example Pipeline Activities:**

1. Data Movement: Copy activity from source to ADLS.
2. Feature Generation: Execute Databricks Notebook.
3. Model Scoring: Invoke Azure ML batch pipeline.
4. Result Export: Copy to Power BI dataset or Cosmos DB.
5. Notification: Send webhook or email on completion.

```
{

"name": "ScoreChurnModel",

"type": "ExecutePipeline",

"typeProperties": {

"pipeline": {

"referenceName": "RunModelScoringPipeline",
```

```
"type": "PipelineReference"
}
}
}
```

## CI/CD for Predictive Pipelines

APPLY MLOPS PRINCIPLES to predictive workflows:

- **Source Control**: Version notebooks, scoring scripts, and configs in Git.
- **Build Pipelines**: Validate scripts, lint code, test endpoints.
- **Release Pipelines**: Deploy models to staging and prod environments.
- **Approval Gates**: Require manual or automated validations before promotion.

Azure DevOps or GitHub Actions can automate this using YAML pipelines, CLI scripts, and REST APIs.

## Monitoring and Retraining

MONITORING PREDICTIVE pipelines ensures they remain accurate and reliable.

**What to Monitor:**

- PREDICTION LATENCY
- Model accuracy (if labels are available)

- Drift in input feature distributions
- Volume of scored records

Use Azure Monitor + Log Analytics to track these metrics and send alerts.

**Retraining Triggers:**

- Schedule (e.g. weekly)
- Model drift detected
- Business KPIs degrade

---

## Governance and Compliance

- TAG PREDICTION OUTPUTS with model version and timestamp.
- Log all inference payloads and outputs for auditability.
- Control access to models using Azure ML roles and Key Vault.
- Use Purview to document datasets and models involved in predictions.

---

## Best Practices

- ◈ USE DELTA FORMAT for intermediate and final outputs.
- ◈ Implement retry logic in orchestration to handle transient errors.
- ◈ Register all models and enforce promotion workflow.
- ◈ Abstract scoring logic into versioned reusable scripts.

- ◈ Validate predictions against benchmarks or thresholds.
- ◈ Log model input/output for traceability and debugging.
- ◈ Automate retraining using scheduled or triggered ADF workflows.
- ◈ Maintain historical prediction snapshots for reconciliation.
- ◈ Monitor and alert on failure, latency, and accuracy metrics.
- ◈ Document the full lineage of features, models, and predictions.

## Summary

PREDICTIVE PIPELINES are the foundation of intelligent applications and data-driven decision systems. With Azure services like Data Factory, Databricks, and Azure ML, you can build modular, automated, and governed workflows that deliver real-time or batch predictions at scale. By integrating model training, inference, logging, and retraining into your data engineering pipelines, you unlock the full value of your data lake—transforming passive data into proactive intelligence that powers business outcomes.

The next section will focus on how to operationalize these models in production, covering deployment strategies, endpoint monitoring, scaling, and lifecycle management for sustainable ML delivery.

# Operationalizing ML Models in Production

OPERATIONALIZING MACHINE learning (ML) models—commonly referred to as **MLOps**—is the process of deploying, managing, monitoring, and maintaining machine learning models in a way that supports repeatable and reliable decision-making at scale. It transforms experimental models into production-grade, secure, and monitored services. On Azure, this involves using services like **Azure Machine Learning**, **Azure Kubernetes Service (AKS)**, **Azure Functions**, **Azure App Services**, **Application Insights**, **Key Vault**, and more to ensure models are scalable, governed, and observable.

This section provides a deep dive into how to operationalize ML models in the Azure ecosystem, covering deployment types, versioning, environment management, API exposure, monitoring strategies, rollback, scaling, and compliance. It emphasizes end-to-end lifecycle management from registration to retirement, and introduces automation practices to help teams continuously deliver and iterate on machine learning capabilities.

---

## Deployment Options for ML Models

AZURE PROVIDES SEVERAL deployment options depending on latency, throughput, and operational requirements.

### 1. Real-Time (Online) Inference

- USED WHEN IMMEDIATE predictions are needed.
- Typically deployed to AKS or Azure Container Instances (ACI).
- Accessed via REST API endpoints.

### 2. Batch Inference

- IDEAL FOR SCORING large volumes of data periodically.
- Executed as pipeline steps or Azure ML batch endpoints.

- Outputs written to Azure Blob, ADLS, or Synapse.

**3. Edge Deployment**

- MODELS RUN ON IOT devices for offline inference.
- Deployed via Azure IoT Edge and Azure ML edge containers.

**4. Embedded Scoring**

- MODEL EMBEDDED IN applications, databases, or Excel.
- Limited to lightweight models or exported ONNX/PMML formats.

---

## Model Versioning and Registry

AZURE ML'S MODEL REGISTRY is the central hub for tracking model versions, metadata, and promotion status.

```
model = run.register_model(
model_name='churn_model',
model_path='outputs/model.pkl',
tags={'stage': 'staging'},
properties={'accuracy': 0.92}
)
```

**Best Practices:**

- TAG MODELS WITH metadata: env, owner, source, accuracy, dataset_id.

- Use semantic versioning: e.g. churn_model:v1.0.0.
- Promote models from staging to production after approval/testing.
- Maintain a model lineage table linking models to datasets and parameters.

---

## Real-Time Deployment to Azure Kubernetes Service

AKS PROVIDES SCALABLE, production-grade hosting for models with autoscaling, load balancing, and integration with virtual networks and private endpoints.

**Step 1: Create Inference Configuration**

```
FROM AZUREML.CORE.MODEL import InferenceConfig

from azureml.core.environment import Environment

env = Environment.from_conda_specification(name='ml-env', file_path='env.yml')

inference_config = InferenceConfig(entry_script='score.py', environment=env)
```

**Step 2: Deploy Model to AKS**

```
FROM AZUREML.CORE.WEBSERVICE import AksWebservice, Webservice

deployment_config = AksWebservice.deploy_configuration(cpu_cores=2, memory_gb=4)
```

```
service = Model.deploy(workspace=ws,
name='churn-service',
models=[model],
inference_config=inference_config,
deployment_config=deployment_config,
deployment_target=aks_target)
service.wait_for_deployment(show_output=True)
```

**Step 3: Secure Endpoint**

- ENABLE AUTHENTICATION.
- Restrict access via VNet or Private Link.
- Store access keys in Key Vault.

---

## Batch Deployment Using Pipeline Steps

```
FROM AZUREML.PIPELINE.steps import ParallelRunStep
parallel_run_config = ParallelRunConfig(
source_directory='batch',
entry_script='batch_score.py',
mini_batch_size='10',
error_threshold=5,
output_action='append_row',
```

```
environment=batch_env,
compute_target=batch_compute,
run_invocation_timeout=600
)
batch_step = ParallelRunStep(
name='batch-score-step',
parallel_run_config=parallel_run_config,
inputs=[input_data],
output=output_data,
arguments=['—model_name', 'churn_model']
)
```

## Endpoint Monitoring and Logging

ONCE DEPLOYED, IT'S crucial to monitor the health, performance, and accuracy of the endpoint.

### 1. Operational Metrics

- LATENCY (AVG, 95TH percentile)
- Error rate (4xx/5xx responses)
- Throughput (requests per second)
- Resource utilization

Collected via:

- Azure Monitor
- Application Insights
- Log Analytics

**KQL Example:**

requests

| where cloud_RoleName == "churn-service"

| summarize avg(duration), count() by bin(timestamp, 5m), resultCode

**2. Model Performance Metrics**

- ACCURACY, PRECISION, recall (if ground truth available)
- Drift in feature distributions
- Outlier detection

Tools:

- Azure ML Data Drift Detector
- MLflow Metrics
- Custom scripts writing logs to Azure Blob or Cosmos DB

## Automated Retraining and Redeployment

DEFINE RETRAINING PIPELINES using Azure ML Pipelines and schedule them via triggers or ADF.

**Example Retraining Trigger:**

- NEW DATA AVAILABLE in ADLS
- Accuracy drops below threshold
- Scheduled weekly/monthly retrain job

**ADF Integration:**

```
{
"type": "AzureMLExecutePipeline",
"typeProperties": {
"mlPipelineId": "retrain_pipeline_id",
"runAfter": ["data_ingest"],
"continueOnError": false
}
}
```

Retrained models can be:

- Registered as new versions
- Evaluated against baseline
- Promoted if metrics pass thresholds

---

## Rollback and Failover

ALWAYS DEPLOY WITH rollback strategies:

- Keep multiple versions in Model Registry.

- Use traffic-splitting (A/B testing) with endpoints.
- Log predictions for validation.
- Revert to previous model version if errors increase.

**Manual Rollback:**

```
model = Model(ws, name='churn_model', version=3)
# Redeploy to endpoint
```

## Security and Compliance

- USE **Azure Key Vault** for storing secrets and tokens.
- Apply **RBAC** to restrict model registry access.
- Enable **Private Link** on endpoints.
- Enable **Audit Logs** for model deployments.
- Encrypt data in transit and at rest (TLS 1.2, managed keys).
- Maintain **SLA dashboards** and uptime metrics.

## CI/CD for Deployment

USE AZURE DEVOPS OR GitHub Actions to automate:

- Model validation and linting
- Deployment to dev/test/prod
- Approval workflows
- Monitoring config updates

**Sample Azure DevOps Release Task:**

```
- task: AzureCLI@2
inputs:
scriptType: 'bash'
scriptLocation: 'inlineScript'
inlineScript: |
az ml model deploy—model-name churn_model—model-version 5—compute-target aks-prod
```

## Best Practices

- ◈ SEPARATE STAGING and production deployments.
- ◈ Monitor latency and error rates continuously.
- ◈ Version models and maintain lineage.
- ◈ Log all predictions with metadata (model version, timestamp, input features).
- ◈ Automate retraining and performance evaluation.
- ◈ Enable autoscaling on AKS for high-traffic models.
- ◈ Use managed identities instead of hard-coded secrets.
- ◈ Perform canary testing or blue-green deployment for critical use cases.
- ◈ Store all operational logs in centralized monitoring tools.
- ◈ Include rollback logic in deployment automation.

## Summary

OPERATIONALIZING MACHINE learning models ensures that AI is not just built, but delivered continuously and responsibly to end users and systems. Azure provides robust tools and services for deploying models in both real-time and batch contexts, with features for monitoring, versioning, security, and automation. By adopting MLOps principles and integrating deployment pipelines into your broader data architecture, you can achieve sustainable, auditable, and value-driven AI delivery at scale.

In the next chapter, we'll shift focus to real-world architectures and use cases, examining how leading enterprises apply data lake and ML integration patterns to drive digital transformation across industries.

# Chapter 8: Real-World Use Cases and Architectures

## Enterprise Data Lake Architecture Blueprint

IN ENTERPRISE ENVIRONMENTS, data lakes have become central to digital transformation initiatives, serving as unified repositories that accommodate structured, semi-structured, and unstructured data at scale. A well-architected enterprise data lake enables cross-functional analytics, self-service data access, machine learning integration, and robust governance, all while adapting to evolving business and compliance requirements.

This section presents a detailed architectural blueprint for building enterprise-grade data lakes on Azure. It walks through the core components of the architecture, best practices for scalability and performance, integration patterns with analytics and ML platforms, data security and governance frameworks, and operational workflows. Real-world implementation examples and strategic design considerations are also included to guide enterprise adoption.

---

### Architecture Overview

AN ENTERPRISE AZURE Data Lake architecture is typically composed of:

1. **Data Ingestion Layer**
   - Azure Data Factory (ADF)
   - Azure Synapse Pipelines
   - Azure Event Hubs / IoT Hub

   - Azure Logic Apps or APIs

2. **Raw Data Storage Layer**
   - Azure Data Lake Storage Gen2 (ADLS)
   - Organized by business domain or source system
3. **Processing and Transformation Layer**
   - Azure Databricks
   - Synapse Spark / Serverless Pools
   - Azure Data Factory Data Flows
4. **Curated and Enriched Storage Layer**
   - Cleaned, standardized, and versioned datasets
   - Delta Lake for transaction support and schema enforcement
5. **Consumption Layer**
   - Power BI
   - Azure Synapse Analytics Dedicated Pools
   - Azure ML and Azure SQL
6. **Metadata and Governance Layer**
   - Microsoft Purview
   - Azure Policy and Blueprints

- RBAC and Access Controls

7. **Monitoring and Management Layer**
   - Azure Monitor
   - Log Analytics
   - Azure Defender for Data

---

## Ingestion Layer Patterns

DATA INGESTION MUST support a variety of data sources including databases, SaaS platforms, on-prem systems, and streaming data.

**Batch Ingestion**

- Use ADF or Synapse Pipelines
- Ingest from SQL Server, Oracle, SAP, Salesforce, etc.
- Schedule or trigger via time or events

**Streaming Ingestion**

- Use Azure Event Hubs for high-throughput events
- Ingest IoT or telemetry data
- Store immediately into raw layer as append-only files

**Change Data Capture (CDC)**

- Use ADF with SQL CDC connectors
- Ingest deltas to optimize data movement

- Version snapshots in Delta Lake

**Example ADF Copy Activity**

```
{
"name": "CopyCustomerData",
"type": "Copy",
"inputs": [{ "referenceName": "SQLCustomerTable", "type": "DatasetReference" }],
"outputs": [{ "referenceName": "RawCustomerParquet", "type": "DatasetReference" }]
}
```

---

## Storage Layer Design

ADLS GEN2 SHOULD BE structured logically to support scalability, manageability, and cost optimization.

**Example Folder Hierarchy:**

/<environment>/ (dev, test, prod)

/<layer>/ (raw, cleansed, curated)

/<domain>/ (sales, finance, hr)

/<entity>/ (customer, order, product)

/year=/month=/day= (partitioned for performance)

**Best Practices:**

- Use Delta format for all curated tables.

- Apply naming conventions and tagging.
- Use Access Control Lists (ACLs) and RBAC.
- Enable lifecycle policies to move cold data to archive tier.

## Processing and Transformation

USE SPARK-BASED ENGINES for scalable transformation jobs.

**Databricks Transformation Job Example:**

```
df = spark.read.format("parquet").load("/raw/sales/2025/05/01")

df_cleaned = df.dropna().withColumn("revenue", col("units") * col("price"))

df_cleaned.write.format("delta").mode("overwrite").save("/curated/sales/")
```

- Apply schema evolution for semi-structured data.
- Use notebooks for development, and schedule jobs with parameters.
- For simple transformations, use ADF Mapping Data Flows.

## Curated Data Design

CURATED DATA SERVES as the canonical source for analytics and ML. Use version control and gold/silver/bronze layering concepts.

- **Bronze**: Raw ingested data
- **Silver**: Cleaned and joined datasets
- **Gold**: Aggregated and business-ready data

**Delta Table Versioning:**

—Query previous version

SELECT * FROM delta.`/curated/sales/` VERSION AS OF 5

- Use columnar formats (Parquet) for performance.
- Partition by common query dimensions (e.g., date, region).
- Enable Z-order indexing in Delta to optimize scans.

## Consumption Layer

ENABLE SELF-SERVICE analytics and data science.

**Power BI Integration:**

- DirectQuery or import from Synapse SQL pools
- Secure using AAD identities and workspace RBAC
- Use shared datasets for report consistency

**Synapse Analytics:**

- Build views and materialized tables
- Define semantic models
- Enable serverless SQL over ADLS with pay-per-query

**Machine Learning:**

- Use curated features in Azure ML pipelines
- Access Delta tables from Databricks
- Register feature sets in Azure ML or Feature Store

## Metadata and Governance

USE MICROSOFT PURVIEW to centralize discovery, classification, and lineage.

**Purview Features:**

- Automated scanning of ADLS, Synapse, SQL
- Column-level classification (PII, PHI, PCI)
- Visual lineage across pipelines and datasets
- Business glossary for data stewardship

**Data Access Governance:**

- Apply RBAC at storage account and Synapse levels
- Use hierarchical ACLs on ADLS paths
- Implement masking in Synapse for sensitive columns

**Purview Scan Configuration (CLI):**

```
az purview account scan create—name adls_scan \

—resource-id <adls-id> \

—scan-ruleset-name default \

—scan-rule-set-type System
```

---

## Monitoring and Operations

MONITORING ENSURES health, reliability, and SLA adherence.

- **Azure Monitor**: Track storage, compute, and pipeline metrics

- **Log Analytics**: Query execution history and failure patterns
- **ADF Monitoring**: Alerts on failed pipeline runs
- **Databricks**: Job run logs, cluster usage, driver logs
- **Synapse**: SQL diagnostics and session activity

**Kusto Example: Failed Pipelines in ADF**

```
ADFActivityRun
| where Status == "Failed"
| summarize count() by PipelineName, ActivityName
```

**Operational KPIs:**

- Pipeline success rate
- Data freshness SLAs
- Cost per GB processed
- Model scoring throughput

---

## DevOps and CI/CD Integration

ENABLE INFRASTRUCTURE as code, automated deployments, and controlled releases.

- **Use Terraform or Bicep** for environment provisioning
- **ADF + Databricks notebooks** in Git for version control
- **Azure DevOps pipelines** for publishing datasets and pipelines
- **Approval gates** for production promotion

**ADF ARM Template Deployment Snippet (YAML):**

```yaml
- task: AzureResourceManagerTemplateDeployment@3
inputs:
deploymentScope: 'Resource Group'
templateLocation: 'Linked artifact'
csmFile: 'armTemplate.json'
csmParametersFile: 'armTemplateParameters.json'
```

## Best Practices for Enterprise Data Lakes

- ⟐ USE DELTA LAKE format for all curated tables.
- ⟐ Apply data classification and lineage with Microsoft Purview.
- ⟐ Secure access via RBAC, private endpoints, and VNETs.
- ⟐ Structure folders by layer → domain → entity → partition.
- ⟐ Automate with ADF, Synapse, and DevOps pipelines.
- ⟐ Track cost attribution using resource tags and workspaces.
- ⟐ Retain data provenance and version history.
- ⟐ Provide data catalogs and business glossary for self-service users.
- ⟐ Schedule periodic revalidation of schema, policies, and permissions.
- ⟐ Monitor data freshness and SLA compliance with dashboards.

## Summary

THE ENTERPRISE DATA lake on Azure serves as the foundation for data-driven innovation. It consolidates siloed datasets, enables advanced analytics and AI, enforces governance, and scales with business needs. With a robust blueprint built around ADLS, Delta Lake, Synapse, Databricks, and Azure ML—alongside tools for governance, monitoring, and automation—organizations can build secure, maintainable, and intelligent data ecosystems. This architecture lays the groundwork for real-world use cases ranging from operational reporting to real-time personalization and predictive analytics.

In the next section, we will explore how enterprises leverage Azure to ingest and process IoT and real-time telemetry data at scale, unlocking use cases in manufacturing, energy, healthcare, and beyond.

# IoT and Real-Time Data Ingestion

THE PROLIFERATION OF Internet of Things (IoT) devices across industries has created new challenges and opportunities in data architecture. From smart meters and factory sensors to connected vehicles and healthcare monitors, IoT generates a continuous stream of telemetry data that must be ingested, processed, and analyzed in real time. Azure offers a suite of services specifically designed to handle the velocity, volume, and variability of IoT workloads, enabling enterprises to build scalable pipelines that support operational monitoring, predictive maintenance, anomaly detection, and other data-driven use cases.

This section provides an in-depth exploration of IoT and real-time data ingestion in Azure Data Lake architectures. It covers the design of ingest pipelines using Azure IoT Hub, Event Hubs, Azure Stream

Analytics, and Azure Databricks, along with best practices for buffering, partitioning, schema enforcement, and storing data for downstream analytics and machine learning.

## Characteristics of IoT Data

IOT DATA IS TYPICALLY:

- **High-velocity**: Thousands to millions of events per second.
- **Small and granular**: Lightweight messages, often <1 KB.
- **Time-sensitive**: Often processed and acted upon in near-real-time.
- **Semi-structured**: JSON or Avro formats with varying schemas.
- **Burst-prone**: Spikes during specific times or due to operational anomalies.

Azure's event-driven architecture is built to meet these demands, offering high-throughput, low-latency, and scalable pipelines.

## Ingestion Architecture Overview

A TYPICAL AZURE IOT ingestion pipeline includes:

1. **IoT Devices / Edge Gateways**
    - Collect and transmit data using MQTT, AMQP, or HTTPS protocols.
2. **Azure IoT Hub or Azure Event Hubs**
    - Acts as a cloud gateway to ingest device telemetry securely.

3. **Azure Stream Analytics or Databricks**
    ○ Real-time transformation, filtering, and enrichment.
4. **Azure Data Lake Storage Gen2 (ADLS)**
    ○ Persistent storage in Delta or Parquet format, partitioned by time/device.
5. **Downstream Consumers**
    ○ Azure Synapse, Power BI, Azure ML, or custom APIs.

---

## Using Azure IoT Hub for Device Connectivity

**AZURE IOT HUB** is a managed service for bi-directional communication with IoT devices. It supports device registration, authentication, and message ingestion.

**Key Features:**

- DEVICE-TO-CLOUD and cloud-to-device messaging
- Per-device identity and access control
- Integration with Azure Event Grid and Azure Digital Twins

**Message Routing Example:**

Route telemetry messages to Event Hub-compatible endpoint for downstream analytics.

az iot hub route create \

—hub-name "iot-hub-factory" \

```
—name "TelemetryToEventHub" \

—source-type DeviceMessages \

—endpoint-name "eventhub-endpoint" \

—enabled true
```

## High-Throughput Streaming with Azure Event Hubs

**AZURE EVENT HUBS** is a big data streaming platform capable of ingesting millions of events per second.

**Key Concepts:**

- **Event producers**: Devices, apps, or IoT Hub.
- **Partitions**: Parallel streams for scalability.
- **Consumer groups**: Independent read views for multiple apps.
- **Retention**: Configurable up to 7 days.

**Event Producer Example (Python):**

```
from azure.eventhub import EventHubProducerClient, EventData

producer = EventHubProducerClient.from_connection_string(conn_str="...", eventhub_name="sensorhub")

event_data_batch = producer.create_batch()

for i in range(1000):

event_data_batch.add(EventData(f'{{"device_id": "device_{i}", "temperature": 22.5}}'))
```

producer.send_batch(event_data_batch)

## Real-Time Transformation with Azure Stream Analytics

**AZURE STREAM ANALYTICS (ASA)** is a serverless engine for real-time query-based data processing.

**ASA Pipeline Steps:**

- INPUT: EVENT HUB, IoT Hub, or Blob.
- Query: SQL-like transformation and filtering.
- Output: ADLS, Synapse, Power BI, or Service Bus.

**Sample ASA Query:**

```
SELECT device_id, AVG(temperature) AS avg_temp, System.Timestamp AS ts
INTO [curated_output]
FROM [eventhub_input]
GROUP BY device_id, TumblingWindow(minute, 5)
```

**Outputs to ADLS (Parquet or CSV):**

```
{
"output": {
"type": "DataLakeStorage",
"pathPattern": "/curated/devices/{device_id}/{date}/{hour}/",
```

```
"serialization": "Parquet",
"compression": "None"
}
}
```

## Real-Time Analytics with Azure Databricks

DATABRICKS PROVIDES advanced stream processing capabilities via Structured Streaming and Delta Lake.

**Example: Streaming IoT Events and Writing to Delta**

```
DF = SPARK.READSTREAM.format("eventhubs").options(**ehConf).load()
json_df = df.selectExpr("cast(body as string) as json").select(from_json("json", schema).alias("data")).select("data.*")
query = json_df.writeStream.format("delta") \
.option("checkpointLocation", "/checkpoints/sensors/") \
.outputMode("append") \
.start("/delta/sensors/")
```

Use **windowed aggregations** and **watermarking** to handle late data:

```
agg_df = json_df.withWatermark("timestamp", "10 minutes") \
.groupBy(window("timestamp", "5 minutes"), "device_id") \
.agg(avg("temperature").alias("avg_temp"))
```

## Storing IoT Data in ADLS Gen2

STORE PROCESSED OR raw data in a partitioned format for scalable access and analytics.

**Recommended Structure:**

/RAW/IOT/DEVICE_ID=123/year=2025/month=05/day=12/hour=14/

/curated/iot/device_id=123/year=2025/month=05/day=12/hour=14/

Use **Delta Lake** for ACID compliance and time travel.

**Schema Evolution:**

Delta allows schema to evolve as new sensors or attributes are added.

```
df.write.format("delta").mode("append").option("mergeSchema",
"true").save("/delta/iot/")
```

---

## Integration with Synapse and Power BI

- USE **serverless SQL pools** to query data directly from ADLS.
- Create views or materialized tables on aggregated IoT data.
- Connect Power BI to Synapse for near-real-time dashboards.

**Synapse SQL Example:**

```
SELECT *
FROM OPENROWSET(
BULK 'https://datalake.dfs.core.windows.net/delta/iot/',
```

```
FORMAT = 'DELTA'
) AS [result]
WHERE device_id = 'device_123'
```

## IoT Analytics Use Cases

- **Predictive Maintenance**: Detect equipment failure based on sensor thresholds and ML models.
- **Environmental Monitoring**: Analyze temperature, humidity, or $CO_2$ levels in real time.
- **Fleet Management**: Monitor vehicle locations, fuel levels, and performance metrics.
- **Smart Buildings**: Optimize HVAC and lighting systems based on occupancy sensors.
- **Energy Consumption Forecasting**: Track and predict utility usage.

## Security and Governance

- USE **per-device authentication** with IoT Hub.
- Restrict Event Hub access with **RBAC** and **private endpoints.**
- Use **Microsoft Purview** to classify sensor data and document lineage.
- Enable **diagnostic logs** for auditing and troubleshooting.
- Store secrets for streaming services in **Azure Key Vault.**

## Monitoring and Alerting

- USE **Azure Monitor** to track Event Hub throughput, latency, and errors.
- Configure **Stream Analytics alerts** based on query conditions.
- Log dropped events and deserialization errors for follow-up.

**Example: Monitor IoT Event Ingestion (KQL)**

```
AzureDiagnostics
| where ResourceType == "EVENTHUBS" and OperationName == "Send"
| summarize TotalEvents = count() by bin(TimeGenerated, 5m), _ResourceId
```

## Best Practices

- ◈ BUFFER EVENTS using Event Hub before processing.
- ◈ Partition and compress files in ADLS for cost-effective storage.
- ◈ Use Delta Lake for upserts, time travel, and streaming integration.
- ◈ Maintain schema registries to evolve IoT payloads safely.
- ◈ Filter and enrich data as close to ingestion as possible.
- ◈ Implement backpressure handling and retries in ingestion apps.
- ◈ Monitor ingestion lag and late arrivals continuously.
- ◈ Apply consistent naming and partitioning conventions.

- ◈ Encrypt data in transit and at rest using managed keys.
- ◈ Document all IoT sources, schemas, and routing in Purview.

---

## Summary

REAL-TIME AND IOT DATA ingestion is a cornerstone of modern, responsive data architectures. Azure's scalable and secure event-driven services make it possible to ingest telemetry data from thousands or millions of devices, transform it in real time, and deliver insights to business users and applications. By combining IoT Hub, Event Hubs, Stream Analytics, Databricks, and ADLS into a unified ingestion architecture, enterprises can unlock real-time intelligence, predictive analytics, and operational automation—driving innovation and competitive advantage at scale.

In the next section, we will explore how to extend these architectures to support hybrid and multi-cloud environments, enabling distributed data processing and governance across diverse infrastructures.

# Multi-Cloud and Hybrid Data Scenarios

AS ORGANIZATIONS SCALE globally and embrace digital transformation, many are adopting multi-cloud and hybrid architectures to optimize performance, reduce vendor lock-in, meet regulatory requirements, and leverage the strengths of different platforms. In such environments, data is often distributed across on-premises systems, Azure, and other cloud providers like AWS or Google Cloud. This distribution introduces complexity in data integration, security, governance, and performance—making robust architectural patterns essential for successful implementation.

Azure provides a broad set of services and capabilities designed to enable secure, scalable, and efficient multi-cloud and hybrid data ecosystems. In this section, we explore how to design, build, and manage data lake architectures that span clouds and on-premises systems. Topics include data movement strategies, hybrid identity and access control, unified metadata management, real-time integration patterns, edge computing, and compliance considerations.

## Drivers of Multi-Cloud and Hybrid Architectures

ORGANIZATIONS ADOPT multi-cloud and hybrid models for various reasons:

- **Data locality requirements** (e.g., GDPR, HIPAA)
- **Latency optimization** for globally distributed workloads
- **Cost management** by leveraging competitive pricing
- **Vendor diversification** for resilience and negotiation leverage
- **Legacy system integration** that cannot be easily lifted and shifted

These considerations necessitate architectures that are interoperable, loosely coupled, and standards-based.

## Core Components of a Hybrid Data Lake on Azure

1. **Azure Data Lake Storage (ADLS Gen2)** – Centralized storage for curated data.
2. **Azure Arc** – Extension of Azure management to non-Azure environments.
3. **Azure Data Factory** – Orchestrates data movement across environments.

4. **Azure Synapse Analytics** – Unified analytics for hybrid and multi-cloud sources.
5. **Microsoft Purview** – Cross-cloud data discovery and governance.
6. **ExpressRoute / VPN / Private Link** – Secure networking to connect clouds and on-prem.
7. **Azure Stack Hub / HCI / Edge** – On-premises Azure-compliant compute for local workloads.

---

## Data Ingestion from Multi-Cloud Sources

AZURE DATA FACTORY (ADF) and Synapse Pipelines support native connectors for AWS S3, Google Cloud Storage (GCS), and other cloud services.

**Example: Copy Data from S3 to ADLS**

```
{
"name": "CopyFromS3ToADLS",
"type": "Copy",
"inputs": [
{
"type": "DatasetReference",
"referenceName": "AWSS3Dataset"
}
],
```

```
"outputs": [
{
"type": "DatasetReference",
"referenceName": "AzureDataLakeDataset"
}
]
}
```

**Key Considerations:**

- Use staged copy with compression to optimize transfer.
- Leverage Managed Virtual Network integration for security.
- Handle data format transformations (e.g., Avro to Parquet) inline.

## Real-Time and Streaming Integration

FOR STREAMING DATA across clouds:

- Use **Event Hubs + Kafka** APIs to integrate with non-Azure producers.
- Use **Databricks** or **Apache Flink** clusters to consume cross-cloud streams.
- Deploy **Stream Analytics** jobs with Event Hub inputs configured from remote connectors.

**Example: Kafka Producer on AWS → Azure Event Hubs**

Use the Event Hubs Kafka endpoint (<namespace>.servicebus.windows.net:9093) with TLS authentication to integrate directly from AWS-based services.

## On-Premises to Cloud Ingestion

### 1. Self-Hosted Integration Runtime (IR)

USE ADF'S SELF-HOSTED IR for secure data movement from on-prem databases.

```
.\IntegrationRuntime_5.0.XXXX.XX.exe /Install /Key:<autogeneratedkey>
```

IR supports:

- SQL Server, Oracle, DB2
- Flat files via shared folder paths
- Windows authentication pass-through

### 2. Azure Stack HCI + Synapse Link

AZURE STACK HCI ALLOWS you to run Azure services on-prem with hybrid linkage to ADLS and Synapse.

Use Synapse Link for SQL Server to replicate operational data directly into Synapse for analytics.

## Unified Governance with Microsoft Purview

PURVIEW ENABLES CROSS-cloud and on-prem metadata management.

- **Scan AWS S3 Buckets**: Using AWS access keys.
- **Scan GCS Buckets**: Via service accounts and OAuth.
- **Register on-prem SQL Servers**: With self-hosted IRs.
- **Link Azure and non-Azure sources**: Into a unified data catalog.

**Purview Scan Configuration (S3 Example):**

```
az purview account scan create \
—name "s3-scan" \
—data-source-type "AmazonS3" \
—resource-id
"/subscriptions/<id>/resourceGroups/<rg>/providers/
Microsoft.Purview/accounts/<account>"
```

## Hybrid Identity and Access Management

### Azure Active Directory (AAD) + Azure Arc

USE AAD TO MANAGE IDENTITY and policy across Azure and hybrid environments.

- **Hybrid Join**: Extend on-prem AD identities to Azure.
- **Azure Arc**: Register non-Azure VMs and Kubernetes clusters for centralized policy.
- **RBAC + PIM**: Enforce least-privilege access to cloud and hybrid resources.

## Edge and Disconnected Environments

IN REMOTE LOCATIONS or air-gapped networks:

- Use **Azure Stack Edge** to process data locally.
- Push filtered/aggregated data to ADLS during connectivity windows.
- Deploy **IoT Edge Modules** with ML models trained in Azure ML.

**Edge Use Case Example:**

- Factory runs object detection using ONNX model.
- Saves defective product logs locally.
- Synchronizes summary data to ADLS at night.

---

## Data Mesh Considerations in Multi-Cloud

WHEN BUILDING A DISTRIBUTED data architecture:

- Treat domains as producers/owners of data products.
- Standardize data contracts and interface definitions.
- Use shared services (e.g., Purview, Synapse) for search, discoverability, and governance.

**Azure Capabilities for Data Mesh:**

- Managed domains via subscriptions or management groups.
- Federated access control via AAD B2B/B2C.
- Centralized catalog with distributed ownership.

---

## Compliance and Sovereignty

ENSURE THAT MULTI-CLOUD and hybrid data platforms comply with legal and regulatory frameworks:

- Use **Azure Policy** to enforce resource location restrictions.
- Store sensitive data in regions with appropriate compliance certifications (GDPR, HIPAA, FedRAMP).
- Leverage **Azure Blueprints** for consistent deployment of compliant environments.

---

## Monitoring and Observability Across Clouds

USE **Azure Monitor** and **Log Analytics** to unify logs and metrics from all sources.

- Integrate AWS CloudWatch or GCP Stackdriver logs via APIs or event forwarding.
- Use Azure Arc-enabled monitoring agents for non-Azure VMs.
- Centralize logs into a **Log Analytics Workspace**.

**Sample KQL for Multi-Cloud Latency Monitoring:**

```
Heartbeat

| where OSType == "Linux" or OSType == "Windows"

| summarize avg(LatencyMs) by RemoteCloud, bin(TimeGenerated, 5m)
```

---

## Best Practices

- ◈ ABSTRACT DATA access through common APIs or catalogs.

- ◈ Design pipelines to be idempotent and resilient to network failures.
- ◈ Encrypt data at all stages with customer-managed keys (CMKs).
- ◈ Use event-driven mechanisms over polling where possible.
- ◈ Standardize schema and metadata tagging across environments.
- ◈ Use Delta Lake for consistent format across cloud and edge.
- ◈ Replicate only necessary data; avoid full copies between clouds.
- ◈ Monitor cloud spend across providers using native tools and FinOps practices.
- ◈ Maintain a central glossary and metadata catalog using Purview.
- ◈ Apply CI/CD and infrastructure-as-code across clouds for consistency.

---

## Summary

HYBRID AND MULTI-CLOUD data architectures offer organizations the flexibility to meet regulatory requirements, optimize cost, and leverage best-of-breed services across platforms. Azure provides a mature ecosystem—featuring ADF, Purview, Arc, Event Hubs, Synapse, and more—for ingesting, governing, analyzing, and acting on data across environments. With strategic planning, architectural discipline, and automation, organizations can achieve a unified, governed, and scalable data lake that transcends cloud boundaries and delivers insights everywhere.

In the next section, we'll explore detailed case studies from various industries that showcase how real-world enterprises implement Azure-based data lake solutions to meet business and technical goals.

# Case Studies from Industry

AZURE DATA LAKE AND its surrounding services have become critical infrastructure components across numerous industries, from financial services and manufacturing to healthcare, energy, and retail. Each sector has unique challenges and goals, yet all benefit from centralized, scalable, and intelligent data platforms that support ingesting, storing, transforming, analyzing, and governing massive volumes of diverse data. In this section, we explore several detailed case studies that illustrate how real-world organizations have designed, deployed, and optimized Azure-based data lake architectures to drive innovation, enhance efficiency, and maintain compliance.

---

## Case Study 1: Global Retailer – Customer 360 and Personalization

**INDUSTRY**: Retail

**Use Case**: Building a unified view of the customer across all digital and physical channels to enable hyper-personalized experiences.

### Problem

A GLOBAL RETAILER WITH millions of customers across online and brick-and-mortar stores faced challenges integrating data from disparate systems—POS, mobile apps, CRM, website interactions, and third-party loyalty programs. The organization needed a single platform to unify this data, apply AI to predict customer behavior, and deliver targeted recommendations in near real-time.

**Solution**

- **Ingestion**: Azure Data Factory ingested daily CSV exports from CRM systems and real-time clickstream data from websites using Azure Event Hubs.
- **Storage**: Data was stored in ADLS Gen2 using a structured folder hierarchy (/raw, /curated, /gold) and Delta Lake for versioned, ACID-compliant storage.
- **Processing**: Azure Databricks handled identity resolution, session stitching, and predictive model scoring.
- **Machine Learning**: Azure ML pipelines trained models for product affinity, churn risk, and dynamic pricing.
- **Consumption**: Recommendations were surfaced in e-commerce and mobile apps via REST APIs hosted on AKS, with dashboards in Power BI for analysts.

**Outcome**

- INCREASED CONVERSION rates by 15% through personalization.
- Reduced churn by 10% via proactive outreach.
- Enabled near real-time campaign adjustment using ML feedback loops.

## Case Study 2: National Energy Provider – IoT-Based Grid Monitoring

**INDUSTRY**: Energy

**Use Case**: Real-time monitoring of distributed grid assets using IoT telemetry to improve uptime and forecast load.

### Problem

THE COMPANY OPERATED thousands of substations and sensors across a vast geography, generating terabytes of telemetry each day. Their legacy systems were not capable of ingesting, analyzing, or acting on data fast enough to prevent outages or optimize grid performance.

### Solution

- **Ingestion**: Azure IoT Hub connected to edge devices and smart meters, streaming data into Azure Event Hubs.
- **Stream Processing**: Azure Stream Analytics aggregated and filtered data in real time, writing critical metrics (e.g., voltage spikes) to Azure Data Lake.
- **Storage and Analysis**: Delta tables were partitioned by device and time, allowing easy querying in Synapse serverless SQL pools.
- **Alerting**: Azure Monitor and Logic Apps triggered notifications for anomalies, with alerts routed to operational teams via ServiceNow integration.
- **Machine Learning**: Predictive models were developed in Azure Databricks to forecast load and detect early signs of transformer failure.

### Outcome

- IMPROVED OUTAGE detection lead time by 40%.
- Reduced maintenance costs through predictive scheduling.
- Supported real-time dashboards with <1-minute latency.

---

## Case Study 3: International Bank – Regulatory Reporting and Risk Analytics

**INDUSTRY**: Financial Services

**Use Case**: Centralized, governed data lake for regulatory compliance, fraud detection, and credit risk modeling.

### Problem

WITH OPERATIONS IN multiple jurisdictions, the bank needed a compliant platform for aggregating transactional data from dozens of internal systems (core banking, cards, mortgages, etc.) and generating accurate, timely reports for regulators. Simultaneously, it wanted to apply advanced analytics to detect financial crime and manage credit exposure.

### Solution

- **Ingestion**: Self-hosted ADF Integration Runtime pulled data securely from on-prem SQL Server and Oracle databases into ADLS Gen2.
- **Storage**: Fine-grained ACLs in ADLS were enforced to meet GDPR and internal data residency requirements.

- **Metadata**: Microsoft Purview was deployed to tag PII and maintain lineage from source to report.
- **Analytics**: Azure Synapse was used for aggregating and reporting risk exposure by customer segment and geography.
- **Machine Learning**: Azure ML models for fraud detection were trained on historical transaction data and deployed to AKS for real-time inference.

**Outcome**

- REDUCED TIME TO generate compliance reports by 70%.
- Improved fraud detection accuracy by 25%.
- Enabled secure access auditing and lineage visualization for internal and external auditors.

---

## Case Study 4: Pharmaceutical Company – Clinical Trial Data Unification

**INDUSTRY**: Life Sciences

**Use Case**: Unify and analyze global clinical trial data to accelerate drug development and ensure compliance.

**Problem**

A TOP-10 PHARMACEUTICAL company ran trials across multiple CROs, each producing data in different formats and at different intervals. Data silos made it difficult to monitor trial health, patient safety, or validate protocol adherence in real time.

**Solution**

- **Data Ingestion**: ADF pipelines ingested datasets from SFTP servers and REST APIs into a raw zone in ADLS.

- **Data Standardization**: Using Databricks notebooks, all incoming data was mapped to CDISC standards (SDTM and ADaM).

- **Governance**: Microsoft Purview captured lineage and ensured that only authorized personnel could access sensitive patient information.

- **Analytics**: BI teams used Power BI over Synapse views to monitor trial progress, identify dropout trends, and track efficacy signals.

- **Machine Learning**: Azure ML models predicted patient dropout likelihood and dosage response, allowing trial adjustments mid-study.

**Outcome**

- ACCELERATED INSIGHTS by reducing data onboarding time from weeks to hours.

- Improved trial protocol compliance through automated monitoring.

- Reduced trial costs by enabling adaptive trial designs.

## Case Study 5: Government Agency – Public Health Data Hub

**INDUSTRY**: Public Sector

**Use Case**: Aggregate, anonymize, and analyze public health data from hospitals, labs, and clinics to inform policy decisions and manage crises.

**Problem**

THE AGENCY HAD FRAGMENTED data pipelines across multiple jurisdictions and struggled to get real-time insights during disease outbreaks or public health emergencies.

**Solution**

- **Data Ingestion**: Azure Event Grid triggered ingestion workflows when hospitals uploaded new data to regional storage.
- **Anonymization**: ADF and Databricks pipelines removed or hashed identifiable data before writing to curated layers.
- **Access Control**: Role-based access in ADLS and Purview ensured separation between identifiable and anonymized datasets.
- **Dashboards**: Regional and national dashboards were built in Power BI with drill-downs by location, time, and disease.
- **AI Models**: Azure ML forecasts supported resource allocation (e.g., ICU beds, vaccine deployment) during emergencies.

**Outcome**

- ENABLED NATIONAL leaders to make real-time policy decisions based on unified dashboards.
- Improved response time to regional outbreaks by 50%.

• Ensured compliance with data privacy regulations across all jurisdictions.

---

## Common Patterns and Takeaways

ACROSS THESE INDUSTRIES, several patterns emerge:

• **Delta Lake and ADLS Gen2** are foundational to most architectures.

• **Azure Data Factory** is the dominant orchestration engine for batch and hybrid integration.

• **Azure Databricks** is preferred for complex transformations and ML workloads.

• **Microsoft Purview** plays a crucial role in governance and compliance.

• **Synapse and Power BI** provide versatile analytics and reporting at scale.

• **CI/CD**, monitoring, and security are non-negotiable in production deployments.

---

## Summary

THESE REAL-WORLD CASE studies illustrate the breadth and versatility of Azure's data lake and analytics platform. From personalized retail and energy grid telemetry to financial compliance and clinical trials, organizations across sectors are leveraging Azure to unify data, derive insights, and drive outcomes. By implementing a robust, scalable, and governed architecture, enterprises can unlock the full value of their data assets and build a competitive advantage in an increasingly digital economy.

In the next chapter, we will examine the future trends shaping Azure data engineering—including emerging paradigms like data mesh and fabric, serverless technologies, and AI-augmented data platforms—offering guidance on how to stay ahead in the evolving data landscape.

# Chapter 9: Future Trends in Azure Data Engineering

## The Rise of Data Mesh and Fabric

TRADITIONAL CENTRALIZED data architectures are increasingly straining under the weight of massive data volumes, diverse data sources, and the growing need for real-time insights across distributed teams. As enterprises seek to scale data platforms while maintaining agility, governance, and business alignment, two paradigms have emerged as transformative forces in the future of Azure data engineering: **Data Mesh** and **Microsoft Fabric**. While the former represents a decentralized organizational and architectural approach, the latter is a new Microsoft product offering that unifies data engineering, analytics, and business intelligence in a single SaaS platform.

This section explores these two concepts in detail—examining their principles, benefits, challenges, implementation patterns on Azure, and how they complement each other. It serves as a strategic guide for data leaders and architects preparing to modernize their data estates using decentralized, domain-oriented, and collaborative data platforms.

---

### Understanding Data Mesh

**DATA MESH** is a socio-technical paradigm introduced by Zhamak Dehghani that moves away from centralized monolithic data platforms toward decentralized, domain-driven architectures.

**Four Core Principles of Data Mesh:**

1. **Domain-Oriented Ownership**: Each business domain owns and manages its data as a product.
2. **Data as a Product**: Data should be discoverable, trustworthy, secure, and usable.
3. **Self-Serve Data Platform**: Shared infrastructure and tooling must empower teams to build, deploy, and monitor their data products independently.
4. **Federated Computational Governance**: Centralized governance policies are enforced via distributed, automated mechanisms rather than gatekeeping.

**Why Data Mesh?**

- REDUCES BOTTLENECKS from centralized data teams.
- Encourages scalability through team autonomy.
- Aligns technical data ownership with business context.
- Embraces DevOps and product thinking in data engineering.

## Implementing Data Mesh in Azure

DATA MESH IS NOT A product, but a way of organizing people, processes, and platforms. Azure offers several tools to support a data mesh architecture.

**Key Azure Components:**

| Data Mesh Layer | Azure Services |
| --- | --- |
| Data Products | ADLS Gen2 + Delta Lake, Azure Synapse, Azure ML |
| Domain Ownership | Azure Subscriptions, Resource Groups |
| Self-Serve Platform | Azure Data Factory, Azure DevOps, Azure Purview |
| Governance | Azure Policy, RBAC, Microsoft Purview, Key Vault |
| Observability | Azure Monitor, Log Analytics |

**Domain-Aligned Infrastructure**

USE AZURE MANAGEMENT Groups and Subscriptions to separate ownership:

- Retail-Data-Subscription
- Finance-Data-Subscription
- SupplyChain-Data-Subscription

Deploy shared pipelines and governance via Azure Blueprints.

**Data Product Contracts**

STANDARDIZE DATA PRODUCT interfaces:

- JSON Schema
- Delta Table Contracts

- Synapse SQL Views
- OpenAPI Specifications for ML models

Enable discovery via Purview:

- Tag domain, product owner, SLO/SLA
- Register lineage and sensitivity labels

## Challenges of Adopting Data Mesh

- **Cultural Shift**: Requires buy-in from business and IT to decentralize ownership.
- **Skill Gaps**: Domain teams need data engineering and DevOps knowledge.
- **Interoperability**: Standardization of metadata, schemas, and APIs is essential.
- **Governance Complexity**: Federated governance must be enforced programmatically.
- **Cost Tracking**: Requires granular tagging and chargeback models.

**Mitigation Strategies:**

- START WITH A FEW motivated domains as a pilot.
- Provide templates and toolkits for data product development.
- Centralize standards and documentation, not control.
- Use Azure Cost Management for domain-level tracking.

## Microsoft Fabric: The Future of Unified Analytics

**MICROSOFT FABRIC** is a fully integrated, end-to-end analytics SaaS platform that builds on top of Azure Synapse, Power BI, Data Factory, and Data Activator. Announced in 2023, it represents Microsoft's answer to the need for a seamless, governed, and scalable data experience across roles.

**Key Capabilities:**

- **OneLake**: A unified data lake based on ADLS Gen2, automatically available to all Fabric workloads.
- **Dataflows Gen2**: Improved self-service data prep with Power Query engine.
- **Synapse in Fabric**: Unified experience for Data Engineering, Data Science, and Data Warehousing.
- **Power BI Embedded**: Deeply integrated BI and semantic models.
- **Data Activator**: No-code event-based alerting and workflow automation.
- **AI Integration**: Built-in support for Copilot and Azure OpenAI.

**Comparison to Azure Synapse:**

| Feature | Azure Synapse | Microsoft Fabric |
| --- | --- | --- |
| Hosting | PaaS (self-managed) | SaaS (fully managed) |
| Storage | Customer-managed ADLS | OneLake unified storage |
| Integration | Modular | Deeply unified |
| Audience | Data Engineers | Engineers + Analysts |
| Governance | Purview + manual | Auto-discovery + lineage |
| Licensing | Pay-as-you-go | Capacity-based (SKU) |

## Implementing Fabric with Data Mesh Thinking

THOUGH FABRIC CENTRALIZES infrastructure, it supports decentralization at the organizational and workspace level.

**Recommended Approach:**

1. **Workspaces = Domains**: Assign workspaces per domain or product team.
2. **Lakehouses = Data Products**: Manage curated datasets using Delta Lake in OneLake.
3. **Pipelines = Product Contracts**: Automate ingest and transformation.
4. **Semantic Models**: Publish certified models for reuse across the organization.
5. **Governance**: Enforce data access via AAD roles and Purview metadata.

## Fabric vs Data Mesh: Complementary Not Competitive

| Concern | Data Mesh | Microsoft Fabric |
|---|---|---|
| Philosophy | Decentralized ownership | Centralized platform, decentralized use |
| Implementation Model | Custom, team-specific | Standardized, pre-integrated |
| Governance Approach | Federated, automated | Centralized with workspace inheritance |
| Entry Barrier | High (requires culture/process change) | Low (SaaS, familiar UX) |
| Flexibility | High (build your own) | Moderate (opinionated patterns) |
| Best Fit | Complex enterprises with mature teams | Mid-size orgs scaling unified analytics |

## Best Practices for Data Mesh and Fabric Adoption

- ⟐ START WITH METADATA contracts and clear product ownership.
- ⟐ Use Purview and naming standards to ensure discoverability.
- ⟐ Avoid one-size-fits-all—some domains may benefit from centralized support.
- ⟐ Design for interoperability: shared schemas, APIs, storage formats.
- ⟐ Embrace automation for CI/CD, testing, and monitoring.
- ⟐ Integrate Fabric and Synapse as delivery tools within a broader mesh strategy.

- ◈ Educate domain teams on data product responsibilities and practices.
- ◈ Continuously evaluate metrics like SLO adherence, product reuse, and domain autonomy.

---

## Summary

DATA MESH AND MICROSOFT Fabric represent two distinct yet complementary shifts in Azure data engineering. Data Mesh emphasizes organizational and operational transformation—devolving ownership to domains and treating data as a product. Microsoft Fabric focuses on technical consolidation—offering a unified platform that empowers business and technical users alike to access, analyze, and act on data collaboratively.

Enterprises that align these paradigms—using Fabric to deliver data products in a mesh architecture—will be best positioned to scale their data capabilities, reduce bottlenecks, and unlock sustained business value in an increasingly complex data landscape.

In the following section, we will explore how serverless technologies and microservices are reshaping data architecture by enabling real-time, elastic, and cost-efficient analytics workflows.

# Serverless Architectures and Microservices

THE FUTURE OF SCALABLE, agile data platforms lies in decomposed, event-driven, and highly responsive systems—enter serverless architectures and microservices. Together, these paradigms redefine how organizations build and scale modern data solutions by emphasizing elasticity, modularity, and developer efficiency. In contrast to traditional monolithic systems or fixed-capacity infrastructure, serverless and microservices support granular control over data services, automatic scaling, and pay-as-you-use billing models—making them ideal for variable, high-throughput data workloads.

In this section, we explore how Azure supports serverless and microservice-based designs in data engineering, focusing on architectural patterns, deployment strategies, key technologies like Azure Functions, Azure Container Apps, Azure Event Grid, Azure Cosmos DB, and microservices deployed via Azure Kubernetes Service (AKS). We'll also examine how to use these patterns to optimize analytics pipelines, implement domain-aligned compute, and achieve rapid, independent delivery of data features.

## Defining Serverless and Microservices in the Data Context

### Serverless

SERVERLESS REFERS TO cloud-native execution models where the cloud provider automatically provisions, scales, and manages the infrastructure needed to run application code. Developers focus solely on the logic, and costs are incurred only when code is executed.

**Azure Serverless Offerings:**

- Azure Functions
- Azure Logic Apps
- Azure Data Factory (Data Flows & Pipelines)
- Azure Event Grid / Event Hubs

- Azure Synapse Serverless SQL

**Microservices**

MICROSERVICES BREAK down applications into small, independent services, each responsible for a specific function and communicating through APIs or messaging systems.

**Characteristics:**

- Each microservice is independently deployable and scalable.
- Built around business domains (e.g., ingestion, enrichment, prediction).
- Often containerized and orchestrated via Kubernetes or similar tools.

## Key Azure Services for Serverless and Microservices

| Category | Service | Description |
|---|---|---|
| Compute | Azure Functions | Event-driven serverless compute |
| Integration | Azure Logic Apps | Workflow orchestration without code |
| Messaging | Azure Event Grid, Service Bus | Event routing and durable queues |
| Containers | Azure Container Apps, AKS | Microservice hosting and orchestration |
| Serverless SQL | Azure Synapse Serverless Pools | Pay-per-query SQL over data lake |
| API Exposure | Azure API Management | Secure exposure of microservices |
| Database | Azure Cosmos DB, Azure SQL Hyperscale | Serverless data storage for microservices |

## Event-Driven Serverless Architecture Pattern

THIS MODEL USES EVENTS (e.g., file uploads, database changes, API calls) to trigger computation dynamically. It suits pipelines where data is ingested asynchronously and requires lightweight, conditional processing.

**Example Workflow:**

1. Blob lands in ADLS /raw/sales/.
2. Azure Event Grid triggers an Azure Function.
3. Function validates and tags metadata.
4. Function calls ADF pipeline to process and store in /curated/sales/.
5. Logic App sends confirmation email or Teams message.

```
import azure.functions as func

import logging

def main(blob: func.InputStream):

logging.info(f"Processing blob {blob.name}")

# Trigger ADF or Synapse logic here
```

**Benefits:**

- Scales with demand.
- Minimal idle cost.
- No need to provision or manage infrastructure.

---

## Microservices for Data Domains

MICROSERVICES CAN BE implemented to isolate logic around specific data capabilities.

**Example Domain-Oriented Microservices:**

- customer-ingestion-service: Accepts batch or streaming data and stores it in raw layer.
- enrichment-service: Adds derived fields like lifetime value or sentiment.
- ml-scoring-service: Receives curated data and returns model predictions.
- audit-service: Logs every record processed with lineage metadata.

Each service:

- Exposes REST/GraphQL APIs.
- Is containerized using Docker.
- Is deployed via Azure Kubernetes Service or Azure Container Apps.
- Logs telemetry via Application Insights.

**Benefits:**

- Independent scaling and deployment.
- Encapsulated failures.
- Team ownership aligns with business domains.

---

## Serverless SQL Analytics with Synapse

AZURE SYNAPSE SERVERLESS SQL pools allow querying data in ADLS Gen2 without provisioning resources.

```
SELECT product_id, SUM(revenue)

FROM OPENROWSET(

BULK 'https://datalake.dfs.core.windows.net/curated/sales/*.parquet',

FORMAT='PARQUET'

) AS sales

GROUP BY product_id
```

**Use Cases:**

- Ad-hoc queries.

- BI dashboards with DirectQuery.
- Data exploration in notebooks.

**Advantages:**

- No infrastructure to manage.
- Pay only for queries.
- Ideal for low-frequency reporting.

---

## Combining Serverless and Microservices

IN MODERN ARCHITECTURES, serverless and microservices often coexist:

- **Azure Functions** act as event-driven controllers for orchestrating workflows.
- **Microservices** in AKS or Container Apps perform long-running, compute-heavy tasks.
- **Service Bus** and **Event Grid** route events across services.
- **Azure API Management** exposes internal services securely.

**Hybrid Pattern Example:**

- A NEW IOT READING arrives → Event Hub → Azure Function.
- Azure Function parses and places metadata in Cosmos DB.
- Function sends event to a Service Bus queue for processing.
- Microservice in Container App consumes the queue, enriches the record, and writes to Delta Lake.

• Azure Data Explorer or Synapse queries the final dataset.

## CI/CD and Observability

MICROSERVICES AND SERVERLESS architectures benefit greatly from automated deployment and monitoring.

**CI/CD Tools:**

- GITHUB ACTIONS / Azure DevOps Pipelines
- Azure CLI or Bicep for infrastructure-as-code
- Docker and Helm for containerized deployments

**Monitoring Tools:**

- AZURE APPLICATION Insights for function telemetry.
- Azure Monitor and Log Analytics for cross-service dashboards.
- Azure Container Insights for AKS/Container App performance.

```
# Sample GitHub Action: Deploy Azure Function

jobs:

deploy:

runs-on: ubuntu-latest

steps:

- uses: actions/checkout@v2

- uses: azure/functions-action@v1
```

with:

app-name: 'ingestion-fn'

package: './'

publish-profile: ${{ secrets.AZURE_FUNCTIONAPP_PUBLISH_PROFILE }}

---

## Security and Governance

- USE **Managed Identity** to avoid hardcoded secrets.
- Restrict microservice and function access via **VNET Integration** and **Private Endpoints**.
- Enforce **RBAC** and **Key Vault-backed secrets** for all services.
- Monitor access patterns and anomalies with **Microsoft Defender for Cloud**.

---

## Cost Efficiency

ONE OF THE CORE BENEFITS of serverless architectures is cost optimization:

- **No idle costs**—you pay only when code runs or queries execute.
- **Autoscaling**—services scale up and down automatically based on demand.
- **Resource isolation**—each microservice can use minimal compute tailored to its function.

For example:

- Use Consumption Plan for Azure Functions with unpredictable loads.
- Use Premium Plan for guaranteed concurrency or VNET requirements.
- Use container instance bursting instead of always-on VMs.

---

## Best Practices

- ◈ USE EVENT-DRIVEN patterns where possible to eliminate polling.
- ◈ Avoid monolith functions—keep logic small and purpose-specific.
- ◈ Treat microservices as products: define clear interfaces and SLAs.
- ◈ Automate deployments with CI/CD from the start.
- ◈ Monitor latency, errors, and cold-start times.
- ◈ Design for retries and idempotency in asynchronous flows.
- ◈ Use Serverless SQL for data exploration; switch to Spark/ Synapse dedicated for heavy workloads.
- ◈ Maintain schema versioning and backwards compatibility.
- ◈ Use standardized logging and correlation IDs across services.
- ◈ Apply Zero Trust principles with network security and identity controls.

---

## Summary

SERVERLESS ARCHITECTURES and microservices are reshaping how Azure data engineers build modern pipelines. These patterns enable faster innovation, better scalability, and more efficient resource utilization—essential in today's real-time, globally distributed, and analytics-heavy environments. By combining event-driven compute, domain-aligned services, and flexible infrastructure orchestration, teams can deliver modular, maintainable, and highly responsive data platforms aligned with both technical and business goals.

In the next section, we'll explore how automation, AI, and large language models (LLMs) are increasingly being embedded into data engineering workflows, augmenting the role of the engineer and accelerating delivery pipelines.

# Automation and AI-Augmented Engineering

THE ROLE OF THE DATA engineer is rapidly evolving. As data estates become increasingly complex, diverse, and mission-critical, the need for intelligent automation and AI-augmented workflows has become paramount. Modern Azure data platforms are now expected not just to support analytics and machine learning, but to also self-monitor, self-heal, optimize, and adapt. This shift is ushering in a new era of data engineering where tasks like data integration, schema management, performance tuning, and quality validation are becoming increasingly automated—guided and accelerated by artificial intelligence.

This section explores how Azure enables automation and AI-augmented engineering through platform features, scripting, monitoring systems, AutoML, data quality services, and the emerging integration of large language models (LLMs). It includes strategies for building adaptive, self-improving data pipelines, and illustrates how engineering teams can transition from manual development to orchestrated, intelligent systems that reduce toil, increase productivity, and unlock higher-order problem solving.

## The Shift Toward Autonomous Data Engineering

HISTORICALLY, DATA engineers were responsible for hand-coding every aspect of the data lifecycle—ingestion scripts, transformation logic, performance tuning, testing, and deployments. In the modern Azure landscape, these areas are increasingly covered by:

- **Low-code/no-code platforms** (e.g., Azure Data Factory, Logic Apps)
- **Infrastructure-as-code (IaC)** (e.g., Bicep, Terraform)
- **Pipeline orchestration tools** with built-in automation (e.g., Synapse Pipelines)
- **AutoML and metadata-driven pipelines**
- **Machine learning and AI for optimization and monitoring**
- **LLMs (e.g., Azure OpenAI)** to assist in coding, documentation, and diagnostics

The result is a growing ecosystem of AI-powered tools that augment engineering efforts, enabling humans to focus on logic and design rather than boilerplate and maintenance.

## Automation Across the Data Lifecycle

### 1. Ingestion Automation

- USE PARAMETERIZED Azure Data Factory (ADF) pipelines for reusable logic.
- Automate schema detection and table creation using metadata files or schemas inferred from sources.
- Enable event-based triggers via Azure Event Grid to launch pipelines upon new data arrival.

**ADF Example: Parameterized Pipeline Trigger**

```
{
"parameters": {
"filePath": {
"type": "String"
}
},
"activities": [
{
"name": "CopyToLake",
"type": "Copy",
"inputs": [
{
```

```
"referenceName": "SourceDataset"
}
],
"outputs": [
{
"referenceName": "LakeDataset"
}
],
"typeProperties": {
"source": {
"type": "DelimitedTextSource"
},
"sink": {
"type": "ParquetSink"
}
}
}
]
}
```

**2. Transformation Automation**

- LEVERAGE DATA FLOWS in ADF with schema drift handling and mapping automation.
- Use Azure Synapse Spark or Databricks notebooks with dynamic parameter injection.
- Store transformations in Git repositories and reuse across domains via shared libraries.

---

## AI-Augmented Data Quality and Validation

AI IS PLAYING AN INCREASING role in ensuring the trustworthiness of data flowing through pipelines.

**Tools and Techniques:**

- **Azure Data Quality Services (Preview)**: Profile, detect anomalies, and define rules.
- **ML-based anomaly detection**: Applied to streaming or batch datasets.
- **Statistical fingerprinting**: Compare current vs. historical distributions.
- **Auto-generated tests**: Use LLMs or heuristic libraries to generate assertions.

**Example: ML-Based Drift Detection in Databricks**

```
from databricks.automl_runtime import load_model

from sklearn.metrics import mean_squared_error
```

```
baseline = spark.read.parquet("/baseline/customer_scores/")

current = spark.read.parquet("/curated/customer_scores/")

error = mean_squared_error(baseline.toPandas(), current.toPandas())

if error > threshold:

raise ValueError("Drift detected")
```

This pattern supports proactive quality monitoring with alerting to teams or triggering fallback logic.

---

## CI/CD and DevOps Automation

AZURE DEVOPS AND GITHUB Actions provide full automation of build, test, and release workflows.

**DevOps Automation Features:**

- AUTOMATED DEPLOYMENT of ADF pipelines via ARM templates or YAML pipelines.
- Infrastructure provisioning using Bicep and Terraform.
- Canary testing and environment promotion for notebooks and models.

**GitHub Action Example for ADF Deployment**

```
- name: Deploy ADF Pipelines

uses: Azure/arm-deploy@v1

with:
```

```
resourceGroupName: 'data-rg'
template: './adf-template.json'
parameters: './adf-params.json'
```

## AutoML and Pipeline Optimization

AUTOML TOOLS SUCH AS Azure AutoML allow users to train models with minimal intervention, selecting the best algorithms, hyperparameters, and feature engineering steps automatically.

**Benefits:**

- REDUCES MANUAL EXPERIMENTATION.
- Ensures consistent pipeline structure.
- Simplifies model retraining in production.

**AutoMLConfig Example:**

```
from azureml.train.automl import AutoMLConfig
automl_config = AutoMLConfig(
task='classification',
training_data=training_dataset,
label_column_name='label',
iterations=20,
primary_metric='accuracy'
)
```

Paired with Azure ML Pipelines, AutoML supports continuous improvement of model quality with minimal engineering oversight.

## Intelligent Monitoring and Self-Healing

SELF-HEALING SYSTEMS are built on top of detailed observability, anomaly detection, and scripted remediation.

**Self-Healing Strategies:**

- DETECT PIPELINE failure via Azure Monitor alerts.
- Trigger Logic App or Azure Function to re-run, clean corrupted data, or notify owners.
- Use historical benchmarks to define healthy performance metrics.

**Example: Alert Rule for Failed Pipelines**

```
ADFActivityRun
| where Status == "Failed"
| summarize count() by PipelineName, ActivityName
```

These alerts can integrate with ITSM systems or webhook endpoints to automate remediation workflows.

## LLM-Augmented Data Engineering

WITH THE RISE OF AZURE OpenAI and GitHub Copilot, developers can now generate pipeline code, SQL, test cases, documentation, and metadata mappings via natural language prompts.

**Use Cases:**

- AUTO-GENERATE SQL queries from natural language.
- Write transformation scripts or notebooks from data specs.
- Document pipeline flows or explain error messages.
- Generate test cases for pipelines and ML models.

**Prompt-to-Code Example:**

"Generate a PySpark script to filter records with null 'email' and write output in Delta format"

Produces:

```
df = spark.read.format("delta").load("/raw/users/")

df_clean = df.filter("email IS NOT NULL")

df_clean.write.format("delta").mode("overwrite").save("/curated/
users/")
```

Such augmentation significantly accelerates development time, especially for junior engineers or business-focused users.

## Best Practices

- ◈ AUTOMATE PIPELINE execution using triggers and metadata-driven logic.
- ◈ Implement dynamic schema handling and format transformations.
- ◈ Use Azure ML AutoML and Feature Store to automate model development.

- ◈ Embed data quality validation at every stage of the pipeline.
- ◈ Monitor pipeline health using Azure Monitor and Log Analytics.
- ◈ Apply DevOps for infrastructure, notebook, and model lifecycle automation.
- ◈ Use LLMs to generate and validate code, tests, and documentation.
- ◈ Build self-healing logic using alerts and serverless functions.
- ◈ Store pipeline metadata centrally for reusability and lineage.
- ◈ Audit and log every stage to support root-cause analysis and compliance.

---

## Summary

AUTOMATION AND AI-AUGMENTED engineering are essential for managing the scale, complexity, and agility requirements of modern data platforms. Azure equips data teams with tools that enable continuous delivery, quality enforcement, performance optimization, and human augmentation. From AutoML to intelligent alerting to LLM-powered development, the future of data engineering is increasingly automated, intelligent, and collaborative. Embracing this transformation will empower organizations to build more robust, efficient, and innovative data-driven systems.

In the next and final section of this chapter, we'll examine how to future-proof your Azure data architecture by preparing for the next generation of tools, platforms, and engineering methodologies shaping the cloud ecosystem.

# Preparing for the Next Generation of Azure Tools

THE AZURE DATA ECOSYSTEM is evolving at a rapid pace, driven by shifts in technology, expectations for real-time intelligence, growing data volumes, and the infusion of AI into every layer of the stack. As the cloud matures, the next generation of Azure tools and services will not only enhance performance and scalability but will also simplify development, improve governance, and make data more accessible to non-technical users through automation and natural language interfaces.

To remain competitive and build sustainable data architectures, engineering teams must anticipate and adapt to these emerging capabilities. This section provides a comprehensive guide to preparing your organization and platforms for the next generation of Azure tools, covering forward-looking architectural principles, investment strategies, training priorities, platform shifts, and the convergence of data and AI.

---

## Strategic Architectural Shifts to Embrace

### 1. From Monolithic to Modular

MODERN DATA PLATFORMS are moving away from large, tightly coupled systems toward modular, composable architectures where services can evolve independently.

**Prepare by:**

- Breaking down pipelines into atomic, reusable components.
- Using containerization (AKS, Container Apps) to modularize logic.

- Moving toward event-driven microservices for ingestion and processing.

**2. From Batch to Continuous**

BATCH PROCESSING IS giving way to real-time and micro-batch pipelines, enabling decisions and alerts based on live data.

**Prepare by:**

- Implementing Azure Stream Analytics and Delta Lake structured streaming.
- Designing pipelines for idempotency and low-latency operation.
- Adding streaming triggers to existing workflows via Event Grid.

**3. From Reactive to Predictive and Prescriptive**

PLATFORMS MUST NOT just report what happened, but anticipate what will happen and recommend or automate actions.

**Prepare by:**

- Building ML models into core data products.
- Instrumenting feedback loops from outcomes into model retraining.
- Using Azure ML and Synapse to integrate AI at every pipeline stage.

## The Rise of Unified and Intelligent Platforms

MICROSOFT IS CONVERGING analytics, data engineering, business intelligence, and AI into seamless experiences through platforms like Microsoft Fabric, Azure ML Studio, and Azure Synapse.

**Implications:**

- **Unified UI/UX**: Engineers, analysts, and data scientists work together in shared workspaces.
- **AI Copilots**: Code generation, data exploration, and insight delivery are increasingly powered by LLMs.
- **Low-code/no-code democratization**: Business users can self-serve complex data workflows.

**Prepare by:**

- Onboarding Microsoft Fabric in pilot domains.
- Defining workspace governance models and naming conventions.
- Upskilling teams on using copilots and auto-generated pipelines effectively.

---

## Investment in Data Products and Contracts

NEXT-GEN DATA ARCHITECTURES prioritize data products—versioned, discoverable, and reusable data assets with SLAs, APIs, and ownership metadata.

**Prepare by:**

- Defining product boundaries within your lakehouse or Fabric workspace.
- Using Delta Live Tables and Data Contracts to formalize expectations.
- Documenting interfaces with JSON Schema, OpenAPI, or Synapse views.

**Example: Sample Contract Metadata JSON**

{

"product_name": "customer_profile",

"owner": "retail_data_team",

"version": "v1.2.0",

"schema": {

"customer_id": "string",

"name": "string",

"loyalty_score": "float",

"last_purchase": "timestamp"

},

"sla": {

"freshness": "15 minutes",

"availability": "99.9%"

}

}

These contracts enable platform-wide discoverability, validation, and consumption automation.

## Infusion of AI and Natural Language

LARGE LANGUAGE MODELS (LLMs) like Azure OpenAI's GPT family are being embedded into:

- Data preparation (e.g., cleaning, transformation recommendations)
- Documentation generation (from schema to pipeline summaries)
- Interactive querying (SQL/Power BI via natural language)
- Anomaly detection, summarization, and root cause analysis

**Prepare by:**

- Integrating Azure OpenAI into developer workflows via API or Copilot.
- Training teams to use LLMs responsibly and effectively (prompt engineering).
- Defining guardrails for AI augmentation in enterprise environments.

## Democratizing Data Engineering

IN THE FUTURE, DATA engineering is no longer limited to specialized teams. Instead:

- Business users define and automate reports or pipelines.

- Citizen developers build apps that consume data products.
- Engineers focus on enabling platforms rather than executing requests.

**Prepare by:**

- Building centralized, self-serve platforms (e.g., via Fabric).
- Educating business stakeholders on data literacy and governance.
- Implementing workspace RBAC, templates, and catalogs.

**Recommended Roles in Modern Teams:**

- Platform Engineer: Maintains infrastructure and templates.
- Data Product Owner: Owns contracts, SLAs, and quality.
- Data Steward: Manages compliance and metadata.
- Domain Engineer: Builds and tests pipelines for their domain.

---

## Automation, Monitoring, and Self-Healing

FUTURE-READY PLATFORMS automatically detect issues, correct themselves, and notify teams only when necessary.

**Key Technologies:**

- Azure Monitor with AI-based anomaly detection
- Data Quality Services (preview) for schema and value validation
- Logic Apps and Functions for remediation automation

**Prepare by:**

- Building observability into every pipeline and service.

- Automating runbooks and incident response.
- Using tagging and lineage to trace errors to their source quickly.

## Cloud-Native and Serverless by Default

ELASTIC, USAGE-BASED infrastructure is essential to support unpredictable loads and simplify operations.

**Prepare by:**

- Moving legacy ETL workloads to ADF or Synapse serverless.
- Replacing always-on VMs with Azure Functions or Container Apps.
- Using ARM/Bicep for IaC to provision infrastructure reproducibly.

**Bicep Snippet: Deploying Azure Function App**

```
resource functionApp 'Microsoft.Web/sites@2021-03-01' = {
name: 'iot-ingestion-fn'
location: resourceGroup().location
kind: 'functionapp'
properties: {
serverFarmId: appServicePlan.id
}
}
```

## Readiness Checklist for Next-Gen Azure Evolution

| Capability | Description | Ready? |
|---|---|---|
| Modular Pipelines | Pipelines broken into services or tasks | ⟐ / ⟐ |
| Metadata Catalog | Microsoft Purview or Fabric Catalog in place | ⟐ / ⟐ |
| Real-Time Ingestion | Event-driven architecture implemented | ⟐ / ⟐ |
| AI-Augmentation | LLMs integrated into development and ops | ⟐ / ⟐ |
| Data Contracts | Defined schema and SLA per product | ⟐ / ⟐ |
| CI/CD Automation | GitHub Actions or Azure DevOps in use | ⟐ / ⟐ |
| Platform Ownership | Teams structured by domain and role | ⟐ / ⟐ |
| Infrastructure-as-Code | Using Bicep or Terraform for provisioning | ⟐ / ⟐ |

## Best Practices for Staying Future-Ready

- ⟐ MONITOR AZURE product roadmaps and preview features.
- ⟐ Adopt modular, cloud-native patterns that evolve with the platform.
- ⟐ Embrace AI as a collaborator, not a replacement.
- ⟐ Train teams continuously in new tooling and practices.
- ⟐ Establish a Center of Excellence (CoE) for data platform strategy.
- ⟐ Keep governance, security, and cost management automated.

- ◈ Build once, reuse everywhere: pipelines, templates, models, APIs.

---

## Summary

THE FUTURE OF AZURE data engineering is one of intelligence, elasticity, and democratization. From Fabric and Data Contracts to LLM augmentation and low-code tools, engineers must prepare not just for new services, but for new ways of working. The next generation of Azure tools will empower organizations to scale analytics capabilities across roles and regions—if they are designed with adaptability, automation, and collaboration in mind.

By investing in modular architectures, robust governance, and AI-enhanced productivity today, data teams will be best positioned to embrace whatever tomorrow's Azure ecosystem brings—evolving not just with the cloud, but ahead of it.

# Chapter 10: Appendices

## Glossary of Terms

UNDERSTANDING THE FOUNDATIONAL terminology is essential for navigating Azure-based data architectures. This glossary provides definitions and context for the key concepts, services, technologies, and patterns referenced throughout this book. Each term includes an explanation tailored for Azure Data Lake and engineering use cases, designed to equip professionals with a precise, shared vocabulary for communication across technical and non-technical stakeholders.

---

### A

**AAD (AZURE ACTIVE DIRECTORY)**

Microsoft's cloud-based identity and access management service. Used to authenticate and authorize users, services, and devices in Azure environments.

**ADLS (Azure Data Lake Storage)**

A scalable, secure, and hierarchical cloud storage service built on Azure Blob Storage. Supports HDFS semantics and is optimized for big data workloads. ADLS Gen2 is the latest version.

**AKS (Azure Kubernetes Service)**

Managed Kubernetes platform in Azure used for deploying containerized applications and microservices. Commonly used in real-time analytics and ML inference pipelines.

**ARM (Azure Resource Manager)**

The deployment and management service for Azure. Enables declarative infrastructure definitions using JSON templates.

**AutoML (Automated Machine Learning)**

A process that automates the selection, training, and tuning of machine learning models. Azure AutoML simplifies model creation for classification, regression, and time series.

---

## B

**BLOB STORAGE**

Azure's object storage solution. Underpins ADLS and is used for storing unstructured data like logs, images, and raw files.

**Bicep**

A domain-specific language (DSL) for declaratively deploying Azure resources, offering a more concise and readable alternative to ARM JSON templates.

**Bronze-Silver-Gold Layers**

A data modeling framework:

- *Bronze* = Raw data
- *Silver* = Cleaned and joined
- *Gold* = Business-ready aggregates

---

## C

**CI/CD (CONTINUOUS INTEGRATION/Continuous Deployment)**

Automated software delivery processes. In data engineering, this includes code integration, testing, deployment of pipelines, notebooks, and infrastructure.

**Cosmos DB**

A globally distributed, multi-model database service designed for low-latency and high-throughput applications. Supports multiple APIs including SQL, MongoDB, Cassandra, Gremlin, and Table.

**Copilot**

AI assistant tools integrated into Microsoft services. In data engineering, Copilot can generate queries, code snippets, and explanations using natural language.

**Curated Layer**

The data lake zone where cleaned, validated, and enriched datasets reside, optimized for consumption.

## D

### DATA FACTORY (ADF)

Azure's ETL/ELT orchestration service. Supports batch and real-time pipelines across various data sources with low-code/no-code integration.

**Data Lake**

A centralized repository for storing structured, semi-structured, and unstructured data at scale. Supports multiple analytics workloads without prior schema definition.

**Data Mesh**

An architectural and organizational paradigm that decentralizes data ownership by domain and treats data as a product.

**Data Product**

A self-contained, discoverable, and reusable data asset that includes datasets, APIs, documentation, and governance policies.

**Databricks**

An Azure-integrated big data platform supporting Apache Spark. Used for advanced analytics, ETL, machine learning, and streaming.

**Delta Lake**

An open-source storage layer enabling ACID transactions, time travel, and scalable metadata handling on data lakes.

**Domain-Driven Design (DDD)**

A design principle where systems are aligned to the structure and language of the business. In data engineering, it supports data ownership by domain.

## E

**ETL (EXTRACT, TRANSFORM, Load)**

A traditional data pipeline approach where data is first extracted from sources, transformed, and then loaded into a target system.

**ELT (Extract, Load, Transform)**

Modern approach where raw data is loaded first, then transformed in the storage layer (e.g., ADLS with Synapse or Databricks).

**Event Grid**

Azure's event routing service that enables reactive programming and serverless architectures through pub/sub semantics.

### Event Hubs

A big data streaming platform and event ingestion service capable of ingesting millions of events per second.

---

## F

### FABRIC (MICROSOFT FABRIC)

A unified SaaS data platform integrating Synapse, Power BI, Data Factory, and Data Activator, all built around OneLake.

### Feature Store

A centralized repository for storing, versioning, and serving features used in machine learning models.

### Function App (Azure Functions)

Serverless compute service that runs code on demand without provisioning infrastructure. Frequently used in lightweight data transformations and triggers.

---

## G

### GOVERNANCE

The framework of policies, roles, and processes that ensure data quality, security, and compliance across the data lifecycle.

### Gold Layer

The most refined zone in a data lake containing business-ready data, KPIs, and aggregates for reporting and consumption.

---

## H

### HDFS (HADOOP DISTRIBUTED File System)

A distributed file storage system for big data. ADLS Gen2 provides compatibility with HDFS for legacy tools.

### Hyperscale (Azure SQL)

A version of Azure SQL Database that allows scaling compute and storage independently for large-scale applications.

---

## I

### IAC (INFRASTRUCTURE as Code)

The practice of managing and provisioning infrastructure through machine-readable configuration files, such as Bicep or Terraform.

### IoT Hub

Azure's fully managed platform for secure, bidirectional communication between IoT applications and devices.

### Ingestion

The process of acquiring raw data from external or internal systems into the data platform.

---

## J–L

### JSON (JAVASCRIPT OBJECT Notation)

A lightweight data interchange format often used in configuration files, REST APIs, and semi-structured data pipelines.

### Lakehouse

An architecture combining elements of data lakes and data warehouses to provide flexible, unified analytics.

**Lineage**

The metadata and tracing information that describes how data flows and transforms through systems.

---

## M

### MANAGED IDENTITY

A service that provides Azure services with an automatically managed identity in Azure AD for secure authentication.

**Microsoft Purview**

Azure's unified data governance solution that enables data cataloging, classification, sensitivity labeling, and lineage tracing.

**Monitoring**

The process of collecting metrics, logs, and traces from services and pipelines to track performance and detect issues.

**ML (Machine Learning)**

A subset of artificial intelligence focused on algorithms that learn from data to make predictions or decisions.

---

## N–O

### NOTEBOOK

Interactive programming environments (often Jupyter-based) used for developing and executing data workflows, ML models, and visualizations.

**OneLake**

The unified data lake in Microsoft Fabric, designed to centralize storage across workloads and simplify governance.

**Operationalization**

The process of deploying ML models and data products into production environments where they can deliver business value.

---

## P

### PARQUET

A columnar storage file format optimized for performance in big data environments. Supports compression and predicate pushdown.

**Pipeline**

An automated series of tasks that ingest, transform, validate, and store data. Can be built in ADF, Synapse, or Databricks.

**Private Endpoint**

A network interface that connects you privately and securely to a service powered by Azure Private Link.

---

## Q–R

### RBAC (ROLE-BASED ACCESS Control)

Azure's authorization system that manages access to resources based on user roles and scope.

**Real-Time Processing**

Processing data with minimal latency to support time-sensitive analytics, decision-making, and automation.

---

## S

### SCHEMA DRIFT

Changes in data schema (e.g., new columns, renamed fields) that occur over time. Handling schema drift is vital for robust pipelines.

**Serverless**

An execution model where the cloud provider manages the infrastructure and dynamically allocates resources. Examples include Azure Functions and Synapse Serverless.

**Streaming**

A continuous flow of data processed as it arrives. Azure tools for streaming include Event Hubs, Stream Analytics, and Databricks.

**Synapse Analytics**

Azure's integrated platform for data integration, warehousing, and big data analytics. Includes SQL, Spark, and pipelines.

---

## T–Z

### TERRAFORM

An open-source IaC tool used to provision and manage Azure infrastructure using declarative configuration files.

**Time Travel**

Delta Lake feature that allows querying data as it existed at a previous point in time using version history.

**Trigger**

A rule or condition that initiates pipeline execution automatically. Triggers can be time-based, event-based, or manual.

**Virtual Network (VNet)**

A logically isolated network in Azure, providing secure communication between Azure resources.

**Z-Ordering**

A data layout optimization in Delta Lake that improves query performance by co-locating related data blocks.

## Summary

THIS GLOSSARY SERVES as a quick-reference companion to the rest of the book. As Azure continues to evolve, the terminology used across teams, disciplines, and documentation grows accordingly. Understanding these terms not only helps in navigating the technical aspects of Azure Data Lake engineering but also strengthens cross-functional communication, enabling more efficient collaboration between architects, engineers, data scientists, and business stakeholders.

In the following appendices, you'll find curated resources for continued learning, hands-on project ideas to reinforce concepts, API guides, and common questions with practical answers to deepen your mastery of Azure's modern data ecosystem.

# Resources for Further Learning

AS THE AZURE DATA LANDSCAPE rapidly evolves with new tools, architectures, and paradigms, continuous learning becomes essential for engineers, architects, analysts, and decision-makers who want to stay ahead. The resources compiled in this section serve as a comprehensive guide to help readers deepen their understanding, develop new skills, and engage with the wider data engineering and Azure communities. Whether you're a beginner seeking structured training or an advanced practitioner looking for in-depth architecture references, these materials will support your journey toward data excellence on Azure.

---

## Official Microsoft Documentation

THE AZURE DOCUMENTATION is continuously updated with the latest service changes, features, and tutorials. Key links include:

- **Azure Data Lake Documentation**

https://learn.microsoft.com/en-us/azure/storage/blobs/data-lake-storage-introduction

- **Azure Data Factory Documentation**

https://learn.microsoft.com/en-us/azure/data-factory/introduction

- **Azure Synapse Analytics**

https://learn.microsoft.com/en-us/azure/synapse-analytics/

- **Azure Databricks**

https://learn.microsoft.com/en-us/azure/databricks/

- **Microsoft Purview**

https://learn.microsoft.com/en-us/azure/purview/

- **Azure Machine Learning**

https://learn.microsoft.com/en-us/azure/machine-learning/

- **Microsoft Fabric**

https://learn.microsoft.com/en-us/fabric/

- **Azure Event Hubs / Stream Analytics**

https://learn.microsoft.com/en-us/azure/event-hubs/

https://learn.microsoft.com/en-us/azure/stream-analytics/

These pages provide tutorials, quickstarts, how-to guides, and reference architectures for real-world implementation.

---

## Learning Paths and Certification Programs

MICROSOFT LEARN OFFERS free, interactive learning paths tailored to various roles and skill levels:

- **Data Engineer Learning Path**

https://learn.microsoft.com/en-us/training/paths/microsoft-azure-data-engineer/

- **Azure Fundamentals (AZ-900)**

A great starting point for understanding the Azure platform.

https://learn.microsoft.com/en-us/certifications/azure-fundamentals/

- **Azure Data Engineer Associate (DP-203)**

The industry-standard certification for Azure data engineers.

https://learn.microsoft.com/en-us/certifications/azure-data-engineer/

- **AI Engineer Associate (AI-102)**

Focused on AI integrations including Azure Cognitive Services and Azure OpenAI.

https://learn.microsoft.com/en-us/certifications/azure-ai-engineer/

These certifications include both theory and practical labs and are widely recognized by employers across industries.

## Books and eBooks

WHILE THIS BOOK PROVIDES a comprehensive foundation, the following additional titles are recommended for deeper study:

- *Azure Data Engineer Associate Certification Guide* – by Jack Lee

A focused guide aligned with the DP-203 exam, including labs and exercises.

- *Designing Data-Intensive Applications* – by Martin Kleppmann

A seminal book on modern distributed data systems and architecture principles.

- *Fundamentals of Data Engineering* – by Joe Reis & Matt Housley

A practical and theoretical guide to becoming a modern data engineer.

- *Data Mesh: Delivering Data-Driven Value at Scale* – by Zhamak Dehghani

The original text on data mesh, organizational structure, and its implications for architecture.

- *Architecting Modern Data Platforms* – by Jan Kunigk et al.

Focused on hybrid architectures, governance, and scalability.

These books complement Azure-specific knowledge with deeper architectural and theoretical insights.

---

## Hands-On Platforms and Labs

LEARNING BY DOING IS one of the most effective strategies. The following platforms offer sandbox environments, real-world challenges, and guided projects:

- **Microsoft Learn Sandbox**

No-cost Azure subscriptions with guided exercises.

https://learn.microsoft.com/en-us/training/sandbox/

- **GitHub – Azure Samples**

https://github.com/Azure-Samples

Repositories that include templates, Bicep/IaC examples, ADF pipelines, and Synapse scripts.

- **DataBricks Academy**

Courses and certification paths related to Azure Databricks.

https://academy.databricks.com/

- **LinkedIn Learning / Pluralsight / Udemy**

Courses ranging from ADF and Synapse to Fabric and Power BI. Use filters to find Azure-certified instructors.

- **Cloud Skills Challenge (Microsoft Events)**

Periodic global learning competitions with certifications and prizes.

## Blogs, Newsletters, and Community

TO KEEP UP WITH RAPID changes, follow reputable sources in the Azure ecosystem:

- **Azure Blog**

https://azure.microsoft.com/en-us/blog/

Official product announcements and engineering deep-dives.

- **Microsoft Tech Community**

https://techcommunity.microsoft.com/t5/azure/ct-p/Azure

Discussions and posts from Microsoft MVPs and product teams.

- **Azure Weekly Newsletter**

https://azureweekly.info/

Curated Azure content including tools, tutorials, and updates.

- **SQLBits, PASS Data Community Summit, Microsoft Ignite**

Conferences with technical sessions on Azure Data Platform.

- **YouTube: Azure Friday, Microsoft Reactor, Data Exposed**

Video content and demos covering everything from SQL to AI.

- **Reddit: r/AZURE and r/dataengineering**

Real-world questions and experiences shared by practitioners.

## Community Projects and Open Source Tools

AZURE DATA ENGINEERS frequently use open source tools in combination with Microsoft services.

**Common Repositories:**

- **Delta Lake GitHub**

https://github.com/delta-io/delta

Used with Azure Databricks and Synapse Spark.

- **Great Expectations**

https://github.com/great-expectations/great_expectations

Open-source data validation, often integrated in ADF/Databricks pipelines.

- **OpenLineage**

https://github.com/OpenLineage/OpenLineage

Metadata standard for lineage across platforms like Databricks, Airflow, and Spark.

- **Terraform Azure Modules**

https://registry.terraform.io/namespaces/Azure

IaC examples for deploying Azure infrastructure.

Exploring these tools builds practical expertise and reveals new architectural options beyond what's in the documentation.

## Specialization Areas and Topics to Explore

ONCE FOUNDATIONAL KNOWLEDGE is secured, consider specializing in areas such as:

- **Data Governance & Compliance**: Deep dive into Microsoft Purview, GDPR, HIPAA.

- **Real-Time Streaming**: Event Hubs, Kafka integration, low-latency analytics.

- **Machine Learning Ops (MLOps)**: Azure ML Pipelines, Feature Store, model monitoring.

- **Data Mesh & Fabric**: Organizational design and domain product development.

- **Security**: Private Link, RBAC, Key Vault, and Zero Trust implementations.

- **Performance Optimization**: Tuning Spark jobs, Delta Z-Ordering, caching strategies.

- **Hybrid & Multi-Cloud**: Azure Arc, ADF connectors, cross-cloud metadata management.

By focusing on specialization tracks, you can align your learning with strategic organizational needs or career advancement goals.

---

## Summary

THIS RESOURCE GUIDE provides a launchpad for continuous learning and mastery in Azure data engineering. From official docs and hands-on labs to community discussions and architectural deep-dives, the Azure ecosystem offers a rich variety of pathways to explore. As tools like Microsoft Fabric, Data Contracts, AI Copilots, and Data Mesh mature, staying engaged with the community and continuously experimenting will keep your skills relevant and your solutions effective.

Whether you're building your first ADF pipeline, designing a cross-cloud architecture, or leading a data platform strategy, the key to success lies in curiosity, consistency, and connection to a broader network of learners and builders.

## Sample Projects and Code Snippets

ONE OF THE MOST EFFECTIVE ways to reinforce concepts and build confidence in Azure data engineering is through hands-on projects. This section offers several sample projects, each designed to reflect realistic use cases across ingestion, transformation, machine learning, and governance workflows in Azure. Accompanying each project are relevant code snippets using Azure Data Factory, Synapse, Databricks, ARM/Bicep, and Azure ML. These examples are modular and extensible, giving readers a practical foundation to implement real-world solutions.

---

### Project 1: Sales Analytics Pipeline with Data Factory and Synapse

**OBJECTIVE**: Build an end-to-end pipeline to ingest CSV data from a secure blob storage location, clean it, store it in curated Delta format, and make it queryable in Synapse Serverless SQL.

**Architecture:**

- INGESTION: AZURE Data Factory
- Storage: ADLS Gen2 (Raw, Cleansed)

- Processing: ADF Data Flows
- Consumption: Synapse Serverless SQL

**ADF Copy Activity Snippet:**

```
{
"name": "CopySalesData",
"type": "Copy",
"inputs": [{ "referenceName": "SalesInput", "type": "DatasetReference" }],
"outputs": [{ "referenceName": "RawSalesOutput", "type": "DatasetReference" }],
"typeProperties": {
"source": { "type": "DelimitedTextSource" },
"sink": { "type": "ParquetSink" }
}
}
```

**Synapse Query Example:**

```
SELECT REGION, SUM(Revenue) AS TotalRevenue
FROM OPENROWSET(
BULK 'https://datalake.dfs.core.windows.net/curated/sales/',
FORMAT = 'PARQUET'
```

) AS data

GROUP BY Region

**Outcomes:**

- PRACTICE DATASET orchestration with triggers
- Understand directory structure and partitioning
- Use Synapse Serverless for ad-hoc querying

---

## Project 2: Real-Time IoT Stream Processing with Event Hubs and Databricks

**OBJECTIVE**: Simulate IoT telemetry data from sensors, process it using structured streaming, enrich with metadata, and store results in a Delta table for analytics.

**Tools:**

- AZURE EVENT HUBS
- Azure Databricks
- Delta Lake
- ADLS Gen2

**Databricks Stream Processing Example:**

FROM PYSPARK.SQL.FUNCTIONS import from_json, col

from pyspark.sql.types import StructType, StringType, DoubleType, TimestampType

```
schema = StructType().add("device_id", StringType()).add("temperature", DoubleType()).add("timestamp", TimestampType())

df = spark.readStream.format("eventhubs").options(**ehConf).load()

json_df = df.selectExpr("cast(body as string) as json").select(from_json("json", schema).alias("data")).select("data.*")

json_df.writeStream.format("delta") \

.option("checkpointLocation", "/checkpoints/iot/") \

.outputMode("append") \

.start("/delta/iot/")
```

**Outcomes:**

- LEARN HOW TO HANDLE streaming data
- Understand checkpointing and state management
- Gain experience with Delta format and time-based partitioning

---

## Project 3: Machine Learning Prediction with Azure ML and Data Lake Integration

**OBJECTIVE**: Train a classification model to predict customer churn using Azure ML, and operationalize scoring by integrating with curated datasets in ADLS.

**Tools:**

- AZURE MACHINE LEARNING Workspace

- Azure ML Designer or SDK
- ADLS Gen2
- ADF for batch scoring orchestration

**Training Script Snippet (Python):**

```
FROM AZUREML.CORE IMPORT Workspace, Dataset
from sklearn.linear_model import LogisticRegression
from sklearn.model_selection import train_test_split
import joblib
ws = Workspace.from_config()
data = Dataset.get_by_name(ws, 'churn_dataset').to_pandas_dataframe()
X = data.drop("churn", axis=1)
y = data["churn"]
X_train, X_test, y_train, y_test = train_test_split(X, y)
model = LogisticRegression().fit(X_train, y_train)
joblib.dump(model, "outputs/churn_model.pkl")
```

**Deployment Integration:**

- REGISTER THE MODEL in Azure ML
- Deploy to Azure Kubernetes Service or as a managed endpoint

- Use an ADF Web activity to call the endpoint during data pipeline execution

**Outcomes:**

- UNDERSTAND MODEL lifecycle from training to inference
- Connect data lake with ML pipelines
- Automate predictions with ADF orchestration

---

## Project 4: Metadata-Driven Data Pipeline Using Purview and Data Factory

**OBJECTIVE**: Build a generic ADF pipeline that dynamically ingests datasets based on metadata registered in Microsoft Purview.

**Tools:**

- MICROSOFT PURVIEW
- Azure Data Factory
- Azure Key Vault
- ADLS Gen2

**Metadata-Driven Parameterization in ADF:**

```
{
"parameters": {
"sourcePath": { "type": "String" },
"targetPath": { "type": "String" }
```

```
},
"activities": [
{
"name": "IngestFromMetadata",
"type": "Copy",
"inputs": [{ "referenceName": "DynamicInput", "type": "DatasetReference" }],
"outputs": [{ "referenceName": "DynamicOutput", "type": "DatasetReference" }],
"typeProperties": {
"source": { "type": "ParquetSource" },
"sink": { "type": "ParquetSink" }
}
}
]
}
```

**Outcomes:**

- BUILD GENERIC PIPELINES that scale
- Use metadata catalogs for discovery and ingestion logic
- Apply security best practices using Key Vault integration

## Project 5: Secure Data Lake with Private Endpoints and RBAC

**OBJECTIVE**: Configure an enterprise-grade data lake with secure access, private networking, and role-based permissions using infrastructure as code.

**Tools:**

- AZURE BICEP
- Azure Role Assignments
- Private Endpoints
- ADLS Gen2

**Bicep Snippet to Deploy Secure ADLS Account:**

```
RESOURCE STORAGE 'MICROSOFT.Storage/storageAccounts@2022-09-01' = {

name: 'datalakesecure'

location: resourceGroup().location

sku: { name: 'Standard_LRS' }

kind: 'StorageV2'

properties: {

isHnsEnabled: true

networkAcls: {

defaultAction: 'Deny'
```

```
bypass: 'AzureServices'

virtualNetworkRules: [

{ id: '/subscriptions/<sub>/resourceGroups/<rg>/providers/Microsoft.Network/virtualNetworks/vnet/subnets/data-subnet' }

]

}

}

}
```

**Outcomes:**

- MASTER SECURE CONFIGURATION of ADLS
- Deploy repeatable infrastructure using Bicep
- Assign storage roles for granular access control

---

## Tips for Extending These Projects

- **Add Logging and Monitoring**: Use Azure Monitor and Log Analytics for operational insights.
- **Enable Lineage**: Register assets and flows in Purview.
- **Add Testing**: Validate data with Great Expectations or custom scripts.
- **Apply CI/CD**: Automate project deployment with Azure DevOps or GitHub Actions.

- **Package as Templates**: Parameterize projects for reuse across teams or environments.

---

## Summary

THESE SAMPLE PROJECTS are designed to simulate real-world scenarios and enable learners to apply Azure concepts in practical, business-aligned ways. By combining data engineering principles with modular architecture, security, automation, and ML integration, these projects offer a blueprint for building scalable, production-grade solutions. As you expand or customize these workflows, continue to use best practices for performance, governance, and reuse—transforming your prototypes into foundational components of a modern Azure data platform.

# API Reference Guide

APPLICATION PROGRAMMING Interfaces (APIs) form the backbone of automation, integration, and customization within Azure's data engineering ecosystem. Whether you're working with Azure Data Factory pipelines, triggering Synapse workflows, orchestrating machine learning tasks, or querying metadata from Microsoft Purview, understanding the available APIs and how to use them programmatically is critical to scaling and operationalizing modern data platforms.

This section serves as a comprehensive guide to the most relevant Azure APIs for data engineering. It includes authentication workflows, example endpoints, request patterns, automation strategies, and tips for integration into CI/CD pipelines or external systems.

---

## API Authentication Overview

AZURE APIS USE **Azure Active Directory (AAD)** for authentication. Applications or users must be granted appropriate permissions (RBAC or API-specific roles) and authenticate using OAuth 2.0.

**Common Authentication Options:**

- **Client Credentials Flow (Service Principal)**
- **Managed Identity (for services like Functions, ADF)**
- **Interactive Device Code (for testing)**

**Python Example: Obtain OAuth Token**

```
IMPORT REQUESTS

TENANT_ID = "<tenant_id>"

CLIENT_ID = "<client_id>"

CLIENT_SECRET = "<client_secret>"

RESOURCE = "https://management.azure.com/"

url =
f"https://login.microsoftonline.com/{TENANT_ID}/oauth2/
token"

payload = {

"grant_type": "client_credentials",

"client_id": CLIENT_ID,
```

"client_secret": CLIENT_SECRET,

"resource": RESOURCE

}

response = requests.post(url, data=payload)

access_token = response.json()["access_token"]

Use this token in API calls via the Authorization header:

Authorization: Bearer <access_token>

---

## Azure Data Factory REST API

**BASE URL:** https://management.azure.com/subscriptions/{subscriptionId}/resourceGroups/{resourceGroupName}/p
Microsoft.DataFactory/factories/{factoryName}

**List Pipelines:**

GET /PIPELINES?API-version=2018-06-01

**Trigger a Pipeline Run:**

POST /PIPELINES/{PIPELINENAME}/createRun?api-version=2018-06-01

**Example Python Trigger:**

headers = {"Authorization": f"Bearer {access_token}"}

response = requests.post(

f"{base_url}/pipelines/SalesPipeline/createRun?api-version=2018-06-01",

headers=headers

)

run_id = response.json()["runId"]

**Monitor Pipeline Run:**

GET /PIPELINERUNS/{runId}?api-version=2018-06-01

---

## Azure Synapse REST API

**BASE URL**: Synapse APIs vary by service (SQL, Spark, Pipelines). Most automation leverages **Azure Synapse Workspace REST APIs**.

**Trigger a Synapse Pipeline:**

POST
/PIPELINES/{PIPELINENAME}/createRun?api-version=2020-12-01

**List all Pipelines:**

GET /pipelines?api-version=2020-12-01

**Example JSON Payload:**

{

"referenceName": "LoadSalesData",

"type": "ExecutePipelineActivity",

"dependsOn": [],

"typeProperties": {

"pipeline": {

"referenceName": "SalesIngestion",

"type": "PipelineReference"

}

}

}

**Spark Job Definition and Execution:**

USING SDK OR REST, submit Spark jobs through Synapse Spark pools.

---

## Azure Machine Learning REST API

USED FOR MANAGING MODELS, endpoints, and experiments.

**Base URL**: https://<region>.api.azureml.ms/

**Register a Model:**

POST /MODELMANAGEMENT/v1.0/subscriptions/{subId}/resourceGroups/{rg}/providers/Microsoft.MachineLearningServices/workspaces/{ws}/models

**Payload:**

{

"name": "churn-model",

"description": "Logistic regression model",

"tags": {

"framework": "sklearn"

},

"properties": {

"run_id": "aml_12345"

}

}

**Deploy Model as Endpoint:**

POST /ENDPOINTS?API-version=2022-02-01-preview

Includes configurations for compute, scaling, and authentication.

---

## Microsoft Purview API

**BASE URL**: https://{accountName}.purview.azure.com

**Search Catalog:**

POST /CATALOG/API/SEARCH/query

**Payload Example:**

{

"keywords": "customer",

"limit": 10

}

**Get Entity by GUID:**

GET /CATALOG/API/ATLAS/v2/entity/guid/{guid}

**Sample Search via Python:**

SEARCH_URL = F"HTTPS://{purview_account}.purview.azure.com/catalog/api/search/query"

headers = {"Authorization": f"Bearer {access_token}", "Content-Type": "application/json"}

response = requests.post(search_url, headers=headers, json={"keywords": "sales"})

print(response.json())

Use these endpoints to dynamically retrieve metadata, lineage, and classifications.

---

## Event Grid and Event Subscription API

USED FOR EVENT-DRIVEN automation (e.g., Blob trigger, ADF trigger).

**Base URL:** https://management.azure.com/subscriptions/{subId}/resourceGroups/{rg}/providers/Microsoft.EventGrid/topics/{topicName}

**Create Subscription:**

PUT /EVENTSUBSCRIPTIONS/{subscriptionName}?api-version=2021-12-

**Payload:**

```
{
"properties": {
"destination": {
"endpointType": "WebHook",
"properties": {
"endpointUrl": "https://<your-function-endpoint>"
}
},
"filter": {
"includedEventTypes": ["Microsoft.Storage.BlobCreated"]
}
}
}
```

---

## Key Vault Secret Management

**BASE URL:** https://{vaultName}.vault.azure.net

**Get Secret:**

GET /SECRETS/{SECRETNAME}?api-version=7.4

**Python Snippet:**

from azure.identity import DefaultAzureCredential

from azure.keyvault.secrets import SecretClient

client = SecretClient(vault_url="https://myvault.vault.azure.net/", credential=DefaultAzureCredential())

secret = client.get_secret("storage-key")

---

## Infrastructure Management with ARM/Bicep

PROGRAMMATICALLY DEPLOY and manage Azure resources.

**Template Deployment API**:

PUT /subscriptions/{subId}/resourceGroups/{rg}/providers/Microsoft.Resources/deployments/{deploymentName}?api-version=2021-04-01

**Payload:**

{

"properties": {

"templateLink": {

"uri": "https://path-to-template/infra.json"

},

"parameters": {

"location": {

"value": "eastus"

}

},

"mode": "Incremental"

}

}

Automate deployments from pipelines using az deployment or REST endpoints.

---

## Security and RBAC API

### ASSIGN ROLE VIA API:

PUT /subscriptions/{subId}/resourceGroups/{rg}/providers/Microsoft.Authorization/roleAssignments/{uuid}?api-version=2022-04-01

**Payload:**

{

"properties": {

"roleDefinitionId": "/subscriptions/<subId>/providers/Microsoft.Authorization/roleDefinitions/<roleId>",

"principalId": "<objectId>"

}

```
}
```

---

## API Tips and Best Practices

- USE **retry logic** and handle **rate limits (429)**.
- Store secrets in **Azure Key Vault**, not in code.
- For high-frequency access, prefer **SDKs** (Python, .NET) over raw HTTP calls.
- Securely integrate APIs into pipelines using **Managed Identity**.
- Validate responses and use logging for every API action.
- Use **Azure API Management** to expose and secure custom APIs.

---

## Summary

MASTERING THE AZURE API ecosystem unlocks the ability to automate nearly every aspect of a data platform—from data ingestion and pipeline execution to ML model deployment and metadata governance. Whether integrating with enterprise workflows, building custom self-service portals, or embedding intelligence into applications, APIs offer the flexibility and power to scale operational excellence. By following the patterns and examples provided in this section, you can confidently automate, extend, and optimize Azure's data services programmatically, ensuring repeatability, reliability, and efficiency across your projects.

# Frequently Asked Questions

BUILDING AND MANAGING modern data platforms on Azure often involves navigating complex tools, services, architectures, and best practices. Even experienced engineers and architects encounter recurring questions around performance, security, costs, integration, and governance. This FAQ section addresses the most commonly asked questions, offering clear, concise, and practical answers based on real-world usage and design patterns. It serves as a reference point for clarifying common misunderstandings and accelerating implementation decisions across data lake and analytics projects.

## What's the difference between Azure Blob Storage and Azure Data Lake Storage Gen2?

**AZURE BLOB STORAGE** is a general-purpose object store. **Azure Data Lake Storage Gen2 (ADLS Gen2)** is built on top of Blob Storage but adds a hierarchical namespace (HNS) and Hadoop-compatible interfaces.

| Feature | Blob Storage | ADLS Gen2 |
|---|---|---|
| Namespace | Flat | Hierarchical (HNS) |
| Optimized for | Unstructured data | Big data analytics |
| HDFS-compatible | No | Yes |
| ACLs | Basic | POSIX-style ACLs |
| Integration with Spark | Manual | Native |

For analytical workloads, always use ADLS Gen2 due to its performance and flexibility for large-scale queries and parallel processing.

## When should I use Azure Data Factory vs. Synapse Pipelines?

BOTH ARE ORCHESTRATION services, but they target slightly different use cases:

- Use **Azure Data Factory** when:

  - Your solution involves extensive movement/transformation across external systems.
  - You need hybrid integration with on-prem data sources via Integration Runtime.
  - You require low-code, visual pipeline authoring for operational data flows.
- Use **Synapse Pipelines** when:
  - You're working within a Synapse workspace and already using Synapse SQL or Spark.
  - You want tighter integration with your data warehouse/lakehouse components.
  - You prefer code-first development using notebooks or scripts.

Functionally, Synapse Pipelines re-use ADF capabilities behind the scenes. Choose based on deployment model and integration context.

---

## How do I manage schema drift in pipelines?

SCHEMA DRIFT REFERS to unexpected changes in source schemas—such as new columns, removed fields, or renamed properties—that can break pipelines.

**Strategies for handling schema drift:**

- **In ADF Data Flows**:
  - Enable "Allow schema drift" option.

- ○ Use derived column mappings to dynamically pass columns downstream.

- **In Databricks/Spark:**
  - ○ Use mergeSchema = true when reading or writing Delta files.
  - ○ Use programmatic schema inference to adapt dynamically.

```
df = spark.read.option("mergeSchema", "true").parquet("/path/")
```

- **Use metadata versioning**: Track expected schemas in Purview or JSON schema registries.

---

## What's the best format for storing data in the data lake?

**PREFERRED**: **Delta Lake**, **Parquet**, or **Avro** depending on the scenario.

- **Delta Lake**: Best for transactional data pipelines, time travel, and frequent updates.
- **Parquet**: Efficient for analytical queries due to columnar storage.
- **Avro**: Best for row-wise serialization (e.g., Kafka, Event Hubs).

Avoid CSV or JSON for large-scale storage except for ingestion buffers. Convert to Parquet/Delta as early as possible in the pipeline.

---

## How do I enforce fine-grained security in ADLS Gen2?

USE A LAYERED APPROACH:

1. **Access Control Mechanisms**:

   ○ RBAC at the storage account level.

   ○ ACLs at the filesystem, folder, and file level.

2. **Network Security**:

   ○ Enable Private Endpoints to restrict access to trusted networks.

   ○ Disable public access.

3. **Encryption**:

   ○ Enable customer-managed keys (CMKs) via Key Vault.

   ○ Audit key usage with Azure Key Vault diagnostic logs.

4. **Purview Integration**:

   ○ Classify sensitive data and apply policies via metadata governance.

---

## How can I track data lineage in Azure?

USE **Microsoft Purview**:

- Register data sources (ADLS, Synapse, SQL DB, Power BI).
- Enable scans to automatically discover and link datasets.
- View dataflows in lineage diagrams: from ingestion → transformation → reporting.

For custom lineage (e.g., notebooks, pipelines), use the Purview REST API to push metadata.

## How do I automate infrastructure deployment?

USE **Infrastructure as Code (IaC)**:

- **Bicep** (native to Azure): Concise syntax, integrated in ARM.
- **Terraform**: Popular across cloud providers, has extensive Azure module support.

**Example Bicep Command**:

az deployment group create—resource-group my-rg—template-file main.bicep

Best practice: Use CI/CD pipelines (GitHub Actions, Azure DevOps) to deploy IaC templates on every environment change.

## What's the difference between Serverless SQL and Dedicated SQL in Synapse?

| Feature | Serverless SQL | Dedicated SQL Pool |
|---|---|---|
| Provisioning | No (auto-scaled) | Manual |
| Cost | Pay per query (per TB scanned) | Per hour (provisioned DWUs) |
| Use Case | Ad-hoc, external table queries | High-volume warehouse workloads |
| Performance | Slower for repeated queries | High-performance data marts |

USE SERVERLESS FOR exploration or low-frequency analytics; Dedicated is for structured, pre-optimized workloads with known patterns.

## Can I use Data Factory to call external APIs?

YES. USE THE **Web Activity** or a **Custom Azure Function** within a pipeline to:

- Trigger third-party APIs (e.g., weather, finance, social media).
- Integrate with REST-based business systems (e.g., Salesforce, SAP).
- Control external orchestration tools.

**Example Web Activity**:

```
{
"name": "CallWeatherAPI",
"type": "WebActivity",
"typeProperties": {
"url": "https://api.weather.com/data",
"method": "GET",
"headers": {
"Authorization": "Bearer <token>"
}
}
}
```

---

## How do I monitor pipeline performance and failures?

USE **Azure Monitor**, **Log Analytics**, and **Activity Run Logs**.

1. **Enable Diagnostic Settings** on ADF or Synapse.
2. Route logs to:
   - Log Analytics Workspace
   - Event Hub
   - Storage Account
3. Use Kusto Query Language (KQL) to create custom dashboards.

**Example KQL Query**:

```
ADFActivityRun
| where Status == "Failed"
| summarize count() by ActivityName, PipelineName, bin(TimeGenerated, 1h)
```

---

## How do I estimate and optimize costs in Azure Data Lake solutions?

1. **Storage Costs**:
   - Use lifecycle rules to move cold data to Archive tier.
   - Compress files using Parquet or Delta.
   - Delete unused snapshots or versions.
2. **Compute Costs**:
   - Turn off idle clusters in Databricks.
   - Use spot VMs and autoscaling in Spark.

- Switch to Serverless SQL for infrequent queries.

3. **Monitoring Tools**:
   - Azure Cost Management + Budgets
   - Azure Pricing Calculator
   - Synapse cost analysis by query

---

## Summary

THIS FAQ SECTION AGGREGATES the most common and critical operational questions encountered by Azure data professionals. From data formats and security to performance tuning, monitoring, automation, and cost control, the guidance provided here reflects best practices drawn from large-scale Azure implementations. Keep this section handy as a quick reference, and adapt the provided patterns and examples to suit your specific environments and workloads. As the Azure platform evolves, so will its capabilities—and a strong foundational understanding will enable you to evolve with it confidently and effectively.

www.ingramcontent.com/pod-product-compliance
Lightning Source LLC
LaVergne TN
LVHW090302210926
848480LV00001B/102
* 9 7 9 8 2 3 1 3 3 6 2 8 9 *